WISE WORDS & COUNTRY WAYS

WEATHER LORE

For my weather-watching friends
worldwide, but especially for Gail
and for Andre (who believes that the
weather is simply a matter of attitude).

WISE WORDS & COUNTRY WAYS
WEATHER LORE

RUTH BINNEY

D&C
David and Charles

A DAVID & CHARLES BOOK
Copyright © David & Charles Limited 2010

David & Charles is an F+W Media Inc. company
4700 East Galbraith Road
Cincinnati, OH 45236

First published in the UK in 2010

Text copyright © Ruth Binney 2010

A catalogue record for this book is available from the
British Library.

ISBN-13: 978-0-7153-3629-8 hardback
ISBN-10: 0-7153-3629-0 hardback

Printed in China by RR Donnelley
for David & Charles
Brunel House   Newton Abbot   Devon

Commissioning Editor: Neil Baber
Editorial Manager: Emily Pitcher
Editor: Sarah Callard
Project Editor: Beverley Jollands
Designer: Victoria Marks
Production Controller: Beverley Richardson
Prepress: Jodie Culpin

Visit our website at www.rubooks.co.uk

CONTENTS

INTRODUCTION

It is impossible to live in Britain without being preoccupied by the weather day by day and even hour by hour. For it affects everything, from our moods to our sports and from farmers' harvests to the state of our gardens. Given the position of the British Isles, set in the north-east of the Atlantic in the path of the jet stream, the weather is always going to be variable, interesting and hard to predict. In April, for instance, on the first day of the cricket season, we may be either basking in warm sunshine or wrapped in winter woollies wondering whether we are completely mad to be outdoors. We know too that the British summer can range from the proverbial 'two fine days and a thunderstorm' to – if we are very lucky – week on week of hot sunny weather.

It is hardly surprising that there are hundreds of sayings relating to the weather and its forecasting. The oldest go back to records made on Babylonian tablets in the 12th century BC, including, 'When a cloud grows dark in the sky, a wind will blow.' The Greeks and Romans also preserved many pieces of weather lore. Foremost among Greek forecasters was the physician Aratus, from whom we get an early version of 'Red sky in the morning . . .' complete with mythological references:

> *Or if Aurora tinge with glowing red*
> *The clouds that float round Phoebus' rising head,*
> *Farmer rejoice! For soon refreshing rains*
> *Will fill the pools and quench the thirsty plains.*

The first weather saying to make an indelible impression on me as a child was the one that my father would come out with every year on 22 December, the day after the winter solstice. He would look up from his breakfast newspaper and pronounce: 'As the days lengthen, the cold strengthens.' Indeed it does, and another of his favourites, 'Ring round the moon, snow soon,' also contains more than a grain of truth. Since childhood I have delighted in and collected such sayings, so it has given me enormous pleasure to research them in greater depth, delving into their origins and their truth – or total fiction! In doing so, I have been helped by one particularly invaluable reference, *Weather Lore*, first published in 1869. Richard Inwards FRAS, its author and compiler, and at one time President of the Royal Meteorological Society, would doubtless have been acquainted with Admiral Robert Fitzroy, Superintendent of the Meteorological Office, who coined the term 'weather forecast' in 1861. On 1 August that year *The Times* printed its first Meteorological Office forecast, predicting fine weather across Britain. However, traditional sayings had to suffice for another 11 years, following a barrage of criticism from the Royal Society.

Among the many other references I have used, two deserve particular mention. One is *The Country Calendar, or The Shepherd of Banbury's Rules*, a reprint of the 1827 edition with a commentary by Professor G.H.T. Kimble. The original sayings and observations of one John Claridge, first published in 1670, resulted from some 40 years of experience and record-keeping, with particular reference to the life and needs of the shepherd. The other is *The Farmer's Friend* of 1947 by W.S. Mansfield, director of the Cambridge University Farm, which combines weather sayings with the up-to-date knowledge of the times. My thanks are also due to Neil Baber and his team at David & Charles, and to Beverley Jollands for her assiduous editing.

Today we are as concerned with the long-term future of our climate as with what the weather will do in the next hour or two. As I write this on a wet and chilly late spring Dorset day, towards the end of the coldest winter for 30 years, it is hard to conjure up the prospect and consequences of global warming. But the weather – and the climate – should concern us all, and while it is amusing to look back to the weather prophets of the past we must also keep our own records of the weather and use them to help become its guardians for the future.

Ruth Binney
West Stafford, Dorset, 2010

CHAPTER 1

COME RAIN
OR SHINE

For all those whose livelihoods depend on the weather, making accurate predictions can make all the difference between success and failure – and even survival. It is therefore no surprise that many weather sayings relate to such occupations as farming and fishing, gardening and beekeeping. Even in the kitchen and dairy it has long been known, for example, that mayonnaise is more likely to curdle in hot weather and that humidity will affect the delicate process of cheese making.

Many of the sayings in this chapter, although they have ancient origins, are not only true – or nearly so – but as relevant today as they were in past times. The lives of sailors are still at risk in stormy weather, and farmers, even with modern equipment such as combine harvesters and electric grain dryers, still hope for good weather for ploughing, haymaking and harvest, although even perfect conditions may not prevent them from complaining. Gardeners, too, know that it pays to take account of the state of the season and, to ensure the best crops, to sow and plant by the weather, not according to the date on the calendar.

Even for those who live in cities, the weather and the seasons can profoundly affect their health. The old saying 'All men are in fair weather happier far' still holds true, as evidenced by the number of people who suffer from SAD (seasonal affective disorder) brought on by lack of sunlight in the winter months. And it is always wise to be prepared, with an umbrella to hand, for rain at any time of year.

FROST YEAR, FRUIT YEAR; RAINY YEAR, FRUIT DEAR

An old adage with some elements of truth – but far from the whole story. Generally the quality of the fruit harvest depends more on summer and autumn weather than on winter temperatures.

As well as frost, snow is also said to be beneficial to fruit, as in the rhyme 'Year of snow, fruit will grow'. While it does not have a measurable effect, cold weather will certainly help to kill off insect pests such as the blackcurrant big bud mite, which can linger during mild winters. Fungal infections, such as silver leaf of plums, tend to flourish when the weather is mild and damp, whatever the time of year.

For fruit, weather conditions are critical at times of flowering, swelling and ripening. If the weather is warm, and the wind gentle, in late spring and early summer, the blossoms will stay well on trees and bushes and have the best opportunity of being fertilized by bees and other visiting insects. Once the fruit has set, then rain is essential to plump it up.

Come the autumn, sun in September helps ripen fruit and turn its carbohydrates into sweet sugars. For grapes, fine autumn weather is also essential to keep away the mildew that can ruin the crop. The only hazard of late warmth is that it encourages wasps to carry on attacking and eating fruit before it is harvested and stored.

A saying first recorded in the 17th century – 'A cherry year, a merry year; a plum year, a dumb year' – reflects the special value of the cherry harvest and its traditional association with life's pleasures (as in 'the cherry on the cake').

The frost hurts no weeds

A saying that is undoubtedly true, not least because so many weeds are able to survive through the winter. What is more, cold weather may even make the seeds of annual weeds more fertile by enhancing their powers of germination.

Whatever the weather, it pays both farmer and gardener to weed regularly to prevent annuals from flowering and making seeds, for as the saying goes: 'One year's seed, seven years' weed.'

In his 1878 lecture *Fortune of the Republic*, the American essayist, poet and philosopher Ralph Waldo Emerson asked 'What is a weed?' – then answered himself: 'A plant whose virtues have not yet been discovered.' The truth, however, is possibly the opposite of this, since many of the plants we now regard as weeds, such as chickweed, dandelions and nettles, were more greatly valued by previous generations than they are today as sources of 'free food'.

Weeds survive the cold in two ways. Some, such as convolvulus and couch grass, reproduce vegetatively, producing underground stems that are ready to sprout as soon the weather warms in spring. Annual weeds, by contrast, produce seeds in profusion during the summer, which lie dormant in the soil ready to germinate quickly as soon as conditions are favourable. And although germination may occur very rapidly after seeds have been shed, continuing the cycle of growth right through until the first frosts of autumn, it can also be delayed for many years. Only when the soil of Flanders was disturbed by the turmoil of World War I did millions of poppy seeds spring to life on the battlefield.

One of the earliest weeds to flower in spring is the shepherd's purse, named from the fact that its fruits are shaped like the purses that shepherds once wore attached to their belts. Like other weeds it was once eaten, as were its close relations the bitter cress and hedge mustard. In praise of the longevity of the plant the poet John Clare, renowned for his intimate knowledge of the English countryside, wrote in 'The Flitting':

And why? This shepherd's purse that grows
In this strange spot, in days gone bye
Grew in the little garden rows
Of my old home now left; and I
Feel what I never felt before,
This weed an ancient neighbour here,
And though I own the spot no more
In every trifle makes it dear.

Who ploughs in April ought not to have been born

Or worse, as this saying often continues, 'who ploughs in May ought neither to have been born nor nursed.' However inclement the weather, all farmers will make sure that their ploughing and sowing are done well before late spring.

The plough is among the oldest of all farming implements, dating back to Sumeria in the fourth millennium BC. Originally it was simply a heavy stick, which was dragged through the ground to make a furrow.

The seasons for ploughing are autumn, directly following the harvest, or mid-winter, both of which give the soil time to be broken down by the frost into a fine tilth that is ideal for germination. Traditionally, the ploughman resumed his work after the Christmas period on Plough Monday, the first Monday after Epiphany, a day recognized by the Church since the 13th century. The day would begin with prayer, asking God for his blessing on the ploughmen's labours.

Later, when work was done, Plough Monday celebrations would begin. Ploughmen from neighbouring farms would decorate their ploughs and drag them from door to door asking for donations. This 'plough money' was used by the parish church to buy candles or 'plough lights', with which to illuminate shrines. It was also customary for the ploughmen to dress up, often in white smocks but sometimes in animal skins, and to blacken their faces. One of the songs they might sing – accompanied by the blowing of bullocks' horns – emphasized the weather conditions they often had to endure while they worked in the fields:

Remember us poor ploughboys,
A ploughing we must go;
Hail, rain, blow, snow,
A ploughing we must go.

The box for collecting money on Plough Monday was customarily rattled by 'Bessy' – a ploughman dressed as a woman and accompanied by another clad as a fool or Beelzebub, the Devil. Bread, cheese and ale, and other food and drink, might be forthcoming from the richer houses in the village.

MACKEREL SKY AND MARES' TAILS MAKE LOFTY SHIPS CARRY LOW SAILS

Good advice, because both these cloud formations are indications of deteriorating weather, and signals for ships to lower their sails as a precaution against damage and even disaster.

A mackerel sky, named from its likeness to the distinctive rippled pattern of dark and light colouring on the fish's skin, is a type of cirrocumulus cloud that forms when there is significant moisture in the troposphere, the lowest part of the atmosphere up to about 16km (10 miles) above sea level. Such a formation is often created as a rain-bearing depression approaches. The gaps in the cloud are formed as it is broken up by choppy winds. That a mackerel sky shows that rain is on the way also gives rise to such sayings as 'Mackerel clouds in the sky, expect more wet than dry' and 'A mackerel sky, not twenty-four hours dry'.

Mares' tails – aptly named small, thin clouds with up-tipped ends, like those of galloping horses – form in cirrus clouds and are correctly associated with high winds; they often appear at the same time as a mackerel sky. Technically called cirrus uncinus, these clouds are distinctive in having no clumps on either side of them.

Sails are no longer a commercial means of propelling ships, but they played a key part in history, powering vessels as diverse as the *Santa Maria*, in which Christopher Columbus sailed westward in 1492, and Horatio Nelson's flagship *Victory*, on which he died during the Battle of Trafalgar in 1805. The age of sail, from the 17th to the 19th centuries, reached its zenith with ships such as the exceptionally fast three-masted tea clippers, whose captains would risk hoisting high sails in all weathers as they raced back to England with the new season's crop of tea from China.

SAFE AT SEA

As well as taking account of cloud formations, sailors would try to avoid storms at sea by observing more fanciful rules:

Never allow an upturned bucket or bowl on board – these are symbolic of capsized ships.

Avoid setting sail on a Sunday.

Fit a ship with a figurehead or paint on an eye to keep evil spirits at bay. Always take note of the warning of the stormy petrel: should the bird fly around the ship, it signifies impending bad weather.

A marriage between two fisherfolk is said to be a sure way of provoking stormy weather.

There is more hay spoiled in good weather than bad

Because in hot weather it can be tempting to stack the hay before it is properly dry, which may even make it ignite if it is not 'turned'. And hay exposed to hot sun can become brittle and low in nutrition.

Meadow hay is simply a collection of any dried grasses and flowers cut from a permanent pasture, but seed hay, a deliberately sown mixture of rye grass and clover, is even more nutritious for feeding farm animals over the winter. May and June are the traditional haymaking months, but in good growing years, with plenty of rain and sun, a second hay crop in late August or early September is welcomed by farmers. The pasture that grows after the first crop is called the aftermath, eagrass or etch.

'There is a tide in farming at every season,' says A.G. Street in his *Country Calendar* of 1935, 'which must be taken as a flood, and especially does this apply to haymaking, although "at the right moment" should be substituted for "flood" in this connection. In other words, when grass is ripe enough to cut, cut it must be . . . a "wait and see" policy at this season leads nowhere save to disappointment and bad hay.'

Haymaking is accompanied by specific customs in different parts of the country. At Ratby in Leicestershire certain meadows were cut on a designated 'Meadow Morning', and the rest of the day spent in amusements. On one estate in Northamptonshire the meadow was divided into 15 portions, each scythed by eight mowers, the leader in each team being bedecked with a garland.

THUNDER WILL MAKE MAYONNAISE CURDLE

And, said cooks in the days before the advent of the refrigerator, it would also make cream and milk turn sour. However, it is still best to make mayonnaise in cool rather than over-cold conditions.

In thundery weather the air is hot and humid – an environment that makes it harder to create the smooth, stable emulsion of oil and egg yolks needed for a perfect mayonnaise. The classic method is to mix egg yolks, lemon juice, salt and mustard then to whisk in oil, first a drop at a time and then in a slow, steady stream. If the oil is added too quickly, or the temperature is too high, the droplets of oil will fail to blend with the other ingredients and the mixture will curdle. In hot, thundery weather, a tried and tested way to avoid this problem is to chill the mixing bowl over ice. To rescue the mixture, and save wasting precious ingredients, the classic remedy is to add another egg yolk while continuing to beat vigorously, although a few drops of hot water may also do the trick.

Thunder is reputed to have other effects – everything from turning tools rusty to making the leaves of clover feel rough to the touch. The first thunder of the year is said to awaken all the frogs and snakes.

The idea of thunder turning milk or cream sour is undoubtedly more to do with the temperature of the air than with the fact that there is a storm brewing. Warm conditions speed the reproduction of bacteria that produce lactic acid, which in turn sours the milk. If left unchecked this process will lead to the milk separating out into curds and whey. In his *Weather Proverbs* of 1883 a certain Major Dunwoody came up with the bizarre notion that 'Increasing atmospheric electricity oxidizes ammonia in the air, and forms nitric acid, which affects milk, thus accounting for the souring of milk by thunder.'

Never offer your hen for sale on a rainy day

Or any other animal for that matter for, as recorded in *The Farmer's Friend*, 'The best hen in the world would be a miserable-looking object on a wet day.'

'Her appearance then,' continues W.S. Mansfield, director of Cambridge University Farm, in his manual of 1947, 'will certainly not commend her to a prospective purchaser.' Advising on the sale of livestock of all kinds, the author comments: 'There is a saying to the effect that "nothing sells so well as condition", and it is true that an animal that carries a certain amount of flesh will look so much better than another of the same sort in poor condition . . .'

The weather is all-important to the health of hens that are free to roam in all seasons. Writing in his series of 19th-century pamphlets entitled *Cottage Economy*, the farmer and reformer William Cobbett is adamant that in winter they 'should be kept in a *warm* place; and not let out, even in the day time, in *wet* weather; for one good sound wetting will keep them back a fortnight. The dry cold,' he continues, 'even the severest cold, if *dry*, is less injurious than even a little *wet*, in winter time. If the feathers get *wet*, in our climate, in winter, or in short days, the do not get dry for a long time; and this it is that spoils and kills many of our fowls.'

WHEN THE CHEESE SALT IS SOFT IT IS SURE TO RAIN

A tip from the dairy, where salt is used in the making of cheese. When the air is damp, and rain is on the way, the salt will become soft as it absorbs water; this is why it is also observed that salt increases in weight before a shower.

> Out at sea, particles of salt can be responsible for the formation of clouds or mist. They are the nuclei around which water vapour condenses.

Salt is used in cheese making, as in other means of food preservation, to kill unwanted bacteria and to stop food from rotting. The farmer's wife or dairymaid would once have used blocks of salt, made by heating crystalline salt and pouring it into moulds. It was then grated into the cheese at the point of working the curd, after the milk had been curdled by adding rennet. As the salt was grated its texture would have been immediately apparent – foretelling the weather.

The propensity of unrefined salt to absorb water from the air means that it needs to be treated in some way to make it pour easily. These days, table salt has an anti-caking agent (such as sodium silicoaluminate or magnesium carbonate) added to it, but an old-fashioned solution was to add grains of rice to grated salt in a salt cellar, to absorb extra moisture and prevent it from clumping.

ALL MEN ARE WITH FINE WEATHER HAPPIER FAR

And women too. In the winter, when levels of sunlight are low, it is a fact that many people suffer from seasonal affective disorder, or SAD. The weather has also played a large part in the art of landscape painters such as John Constable.

Seasonal affective disorder is a cause of 'winter blues', which can range from mild loss of energy to disabling lethargy and depression. It occurs when insufficient light reaches the hypothalamus, the part of the brain that controls such functions as sleep, appetite, sex drive and mood. To treat the problem it is possible to obtain lamps that provide so-called 'full spectrum light'. When used for some four hours a day they can alleviate many of the symptoms of SAD.

In summer, endless days of rain can produce similar emotions, although they have no medical label. To the pessimistic they are the proof that 'it never rains but it pours'. In a soggy summer there is little to do but seek pleasure in indoor amusements. In the 17th century a collection of proverbs by James Howell included the line: 'Raine, raine goe to Spain: faire weather come againe.' In 1687 the antiquary and biographer John Aubrey wrote that little children, 'to charme away the Raine', used this rhyme:

> Rain raine goe away
> Come again a Saturday.

Since Aubrey's time the last line has been subject to many variations – from 'Come again another day' to 'Little Arthur wants to play'.

From his first detailed weather observations in 1806, Constable was aware of the influence that the sky would have on his work. He believed that the sky was the 'source of light that governs everything' and 'the chief organ of sentiment'. His relationship with the sky led to a totally new approach to landscape painting; between 1820 and 1822 he created 51 studies that were 'pure sky' – with no visible landscape in them at all.

When the wind is in the south, it blows the bait in the fish's mouth

An old adage for fishermen, predicting the best conditions for making a catch. Other aspects of the elements and the seasons are also crucial to successful fishing.

The great exponent of fly fishing, Izaac Walton, had plenty to say about the effect of the wind direction. 'Next to the south wind,' he writes in *The Compleat Angler*, first published in 1653, 'the west wind is believed to be the best' and the east wind the worst. However, he continues, '. . . if it be a cloudy day, and not extreme cold' (that is, ideal fishing conditions) 'let the wind set in what corner it will and do its worst, I heed it not.'

The position of the angler relative to the wind is also important. Describing a perfect technique for fly fishing, Walton advises: '. . . before you begin to angle cast to have the wind on your back; and the sun, if it shines, to be before you; and to fish down the stream; and carry the point or top of your rod downward, by which means, the shadow of yourself and rod will be least offensive to the fish . . .'

As to bait, anglers are known to use everything from worms to pieces of cheese to lure their catch, but may vary their choice with the seasons. Advising on bait suitable for catching chub, Walton says: '. . . you are to note that in March and April he is usually taken with worms; in May, June, and July he will bite at any fly, or at cherries, or at beetles with their legs and wings cut off, or at any kind of snail, or at the black bee that breeds in clay walls; and he never refuses a grasshopper, on the top of a swift stream . . . In August, and in the cooler months, a yellow paste made of the strongest cheese, and pounded in a mortar, with a little butter and saffron, so much of it, as being beaten small, will turn it to a lemon colour.'

The avid angler will fish whatever the weather, as this verse from the 17th-century poet John Chalkhill confirms (gentles are a type of red worm):

> *We have gentles in a horn,*
> > *We have paste and worms too;*
> *We can watch both night and morn,*
> > *Suffer rain and storms too.*
> > *None do here*
> > *Use to swear,*
> > *Oaths do fray*
> > *Fish away*
> > *We sit still*
> > *And watch our quill:*
> *Fishers must not wrangle.*

THE BLACKSMITH WORKS BEST ON A STORMY DAY

Because, it is said, the fire of the smithy's forge burns brighter and with more heat when a storm is due. The craft of the blacksmith has been revered since ancient times and, like fire itself, is associated with other lore.

Blacksmiths depend on the heat of a fire to soften metal sufficiently so that it can be worked. Crucial to this is oxygen, without which wood or coal will not burn. With wind – as anyone who has ever made a bonfire knows – more oxygen is delivered and the fuel flames well, with a good heat.

Although a stormy day might help their fires, country blacksmiths believed that iron would not weld properly when lightning was about. However, they also held to the notion that water that had been struck by lightning was particularly good for tempering iron, so they would empty their cooling troughs after a storm and refill them with newly fallen rainwater.

BURNING BRIGHT

Watch a fire – and read the weather – because it is said that:

Sunshine will put out a fire.

A fire that is hard to kindle indicates bad weather.

A fire crackling gently is 'treading snow'.

Coals covered with thick white ashes indicate snow in winter and rain in summer.

If burning coals stick to the bottom of a pot, it is a sign of a tempest.

When the wind is in the North, the skilful fisher goes not forth

Rightly, because his catch will be small and he may risk his life getting it. In the winter, however, a north wind, despite being cold, can in fact be associated with fair weather, and it has been discovered that wind blowing across the ocean can have an advantageous effect on fish stocks.

The reasons why those fishing with rod and line on the bank of a river or lake should beware of north winds are expressed in the verse:

> *Fishermen in anger froth*
> *When the wind is in the north;*
> *For fish bite the best*
> *When the wind is in the west.*

In other words, fish will not bite when the wind is northerly.

However, wind from any direction can be beneficial to sea fishermen because – as was noticed by the Norwegian explorer Fridtjof Nansen when he was sailing between drifting icebergs in the Arctic in the 1890s, and subsequently explained by the Swedish oceanographer Vagn Walfrid Ekman – the sea moves at a 45° angle to the wind. As it does so, it drives surface currents downwards to depths of several hundred metres; these then drag up water containing large quantities of nutrients on which plankton feed and in turn attract large fish such as cod.

> *In the dairy it is said that 'Cream makes most freely with a north wind.'*

People in other occupations should also take note of the wind, although the advice can be contradictory. Pliny, for instance, says: 'Take care not to sow in a north wind, or to graft and inoculate when the wind is in the south.' But the 17th-century gardener John Worledge advises that 'The north wind is best for sowing of seed, the south for grafting.'

THE NORTH WIND – GOOD AND BAD

Any weather watcher can take their pick from a variety of sayings about the north wind:

'The north wind [brings] wet and cold together.' (*Satire on the Humid Climate of the British Isles*)

'The north wind bringeth forth rain.' (Proverbs, Ch 25, v 23).

'Speaking generally, a year with the wind from the north is better and more healthy than one with wind from the south.' (Theophrastus)

'To run upon the sharp wind of the north,
To do me business in the veins o' the earth
When it is bak'd with frost.'
(Shakespeare, *The Tempest*)

'The north wind makes men more cheerful and begets a better appetite to meat.' (John Worlidge, 1669)

Dry your barley in october, or you'll always be sober

That is, you will never have enough barley to make an alcoholic drink – or enough money to buy a drink for yourself or even a friend. If not properly dried before it is stored, barley will quickly rot and so fail both as an animal feed and a key ingredient of beer, barley wine and whisky.

Although barley originated in the Middle East, having first been cultivated in Syria some 10,000 years ago, for about 8,000 years it was the principle grain crop of Europe, being made into bread, porridge, beer and barley water, until it was superseded by wheat. Pliny, in his *Natural History* of the first century AD, called barley 'the oldest food' and described granaries designed for drying it, with 'brick walls a yard thick', filled from above and both 'draught-proof and windowless'. Another type, made from wood, were supported on pillars so that the air could circulate 'on all sides and even from below'.

Today, thanks to its hardiness and ability to mature quickly, barley is chiefly a crop of more temperate climes, being sown both in autumn, to overwinter, and in spring. By October most of the crop should be mature and the farmer will hope for good drying weather in a month that can be extremely wet.

The first beer was probably made in Mesopotamia by soaking barley cakes in water and allowing the mixture to ferment, but a more alcoholic beverage resulted when the barley grains were first germinated then dried and heated to produce malt, a sugar that produced not only a more powerful fermentation but also a much better flavour. Barley wine is a relatively new name (dating to 1903) for strong ales matured in wooden barrels, often for several years.

> The distillation of malted barley produces whisky, the drink that the Celts called *uisge beatha* or 'water of life'. In Scotland it became customary to dry the barley over a peat fire, imparting a characteristically smoky taste.

A WISE MAN CARRIES HIS CLOAK IN FAIR WEATHER, AND A FOOL WANTS HIS IN RAIN

And a sensible man or women will take an umbrella also. Such are the vagaries of the Northern European climate that similar sentiments are expressed well beyond British shores.

Wool, being rich in lanolin, is reasonably weatherproof, and for centuries those who ventured out in adverse conditions did so in woollen cloaks or greatcoats. It was not until the 19th century that the raincoat was invented. In 1823 the Scottish chemist Charles Macintosh sandwiched a layer of rubber dissolved in coal tar (a by-product from gasworks) between two pieces of cloth to make waterproof fabric. The biggest problems with the new material were its offensive smell and the fact that in cold weather it was stiff and crackly while in the heat it became sticky. Matters improved in 1839 when Charles Goodyear invented vulcanized rubber by adding sulphur to the raw material, which increased its stability and elasticity.

A different method of weatherproofing was invented by Thomas Burberry: he treated cotton yarn with a chemical water repellent then used it to create a tightly woven twill fabric, which he called gabardine. Following its launch in 1880, the gabardine raincoat became a standard item for both the fashionable and, in the form of the trench coat, for soldiers.

As to the necessity of carrying an umbrella, the Victorian manual *Enquire Within* was adamant: 'If the weather appears doubtful,' it says, 'always take the precaution of having an umbrella when you go out, as you thereby avoid the chance of getting wet – or encroaching under a friend's umbrella – or being under the necessity of borrowing one, which involves the trouble of returning it, and possibly puts the lender to inconvenience.'

The collapsible umbrella, probably invented by the Chinese around 1000 BC, was originally made of bamboo covered in silk and was probably not waterproof, but by the sixth century AD the Chinese were using oiled mulberry bark, which was indeed rain-resistant.

For the ancient Chinese, putting up an umbrella indoors was believed to be an insult to the sun, which they worshipped as a deity. In Britain the very fact of opening an umbrella at all was once thought to be ungodly. The philanthropist Jonas Hanway, who regularly used one from the 1750s, is said to have been the first Londoner to break the taboo. Clerics of the time maintained it was the Lord's purpose that people should get wet if it rained.

UMBRELLA LORE

As well as those concerning opening them indoors, many other superstitions relate to both umbrellas and sunshades:

It is unlucky to give someone an umbrella as a gift, or to put an umbrella on the bed.

If you drop an umbrella, do not pick it up. Let someone else do so and you will avert evil omens. On no account should you thank them.

The person who picks up another's dropped umbrella will themselves attract good fortune.

THOUGH IT RAINS, DO NOT NEGLECT TO WATER

Good advice for the gardener, who also needs to rely on the watering can when weeding, thinning and transplanting.

The careful gardener will collect and store rainwater for use when carrying out these essential gardening tasks, and will be sure to water plants well. If there is insufficient moisture to penetrate the soil deeply, plants will develop shallow roots, which not

> *To make the most of the rain, it helps to compost well and to mulch the soil thoroughly after rain so as to retain as much water in the soil as possible.*

only make them liable to wind damage but decrease their capacity to absorb nutrients.

When transplanting, plenty of water is essential to help cushion plants from the shock of being moved. It is said that you should transplant when it is raining, but failing this a good method is to make a hole with a dibber or trowel and to add water to the hole before planting.

The water butt, originally made of wood, has long been a feature of the well-managed garden. Rainwater would also be collected in pools, ponds and channels constructed between raised beds. When using rainwater, the watering can is the ideal receptacle. Early ones, made from the 1470s onwards, were simply vase-shaped clay pots with holes in the base.

IF BEES SWARM IN MAY, THEY'RE WORTH A POUND NEXT DAY

Or maybe even a load of hay. Bee-keepers have always favoured early (though not premature) swarms, and the behaviour of bees is also regarded as a key to weather prediction at other times of the year.

Honey bees swarm to increase their numbers. In late spring the young queens are ready to fly from the hive while, at the same time, the workers become restless, gathering at the hive entrance ready to raid the honey cells for food. When the queen emerges, about half the workers cluster around her, then swarm as she flies off. If she has already been impregnated by a drone, the swarm will seek a new home; if not she may return to the hive. There is a well-known rhyme about swarming bees, which runs:

> A swarm of bees in May is worth a load of hay,
> A swarm of bees in June is worth a silver spoon,
> A swarm of bees in July is not worth a fly.

In other words, by midsummer the value of the swarm is minimal.

Over the winter, bees huddle together within the hive for warmth. By early February they are beginning to rear new broods, but if they swarm too early – for example in sudden sunny spells in February or March – they may jeopardize their chance of establishing themselves and making enough honey for the colony to survive.

BEE FORECASTS

Some of the many sayings that relate to bee behaviour:

If bees stay at home,
Rain will soon come;
If they fly away,
Fine will be the day.

Bees early at work will not go on all day.

Bees will not swarm
Before a storm.

When many bees enter the hive and none leave it, rain is near.

Changes in the weather put pigs off their food

While a pig carrying straw in its mouth is believed to be a sign of rain. Pigs are also thought to be able to 'see' the wind and even to propitiate ghosts.

Pigs are intelligent animals which, when kept outdoors, are able to respond to changes in the weather. Probably because of their acute sense of hearing, they greatly dislike wind, as Francis Bacon observed: 'Swine are so terrified and disturbed and discomposed when the wind is getting up, that countrymen say that this animal alone sees the wind, and that it must be frightful to look at.' When a storm is coming, they will pick up straw in their mouths and take it to their sties. In fair, weather, however, they enjoy rolling in the mud, as this rhyme confirms:

When pigs carry sticks,
The clouds will play tricks;
When they lie in the mud,
No fears of flood.

The behaviour of pigs is integral to a Scottish account of so-called 'borrowing days'. Because the beginning of April is often stormy, the first three days of the month are said

to be borrowed from the end of March. The early 19th-century verse by John Jamieson runs:

> *March said to Aperill:*
> *I saw three hogs upon a hill;*
> *But lend your first three days to me,*
> *And I'll be bound to gar them die.*
> *The first, it shall be wind and weet;*
> *The next it shall be snaw and sleet;*
> *The third it shall be sic a freeze*
> *Shall gar the birds stick to the trees –*
> *But when the borrowed days were gane,*
> *The three silly hogs came hirplin hame.*

Because of the pig's sensitivity to changing weather, its squeal was once believed to be able to dissipate the light from St Elmo's fire (see page 166). In the days when people feared eclipses, they would grunt like pigs to protect themselves from danger.

A RED EVENING AND A GREY MORNING SETS THE PILGRIM WALKING

Such a combination of weather signs is a likely forecast of a fine day, so is good for anyone needing to be outdoors, including pilgrims.

Pilgrimage is an ancient ritual associated with spiritual renewal and healing, and is a feature of both Christianity and Islam, while Australian aborigines have been making pilgrimages to Uluru (Ayer's Rock) for at least 10,000 years. For Christians, spring, the season of Easter, is the most popular time for pilgrimage, although the weather can be cold, even along the routes to such sites as Santiago de Compostela.

In *The Canterbury Tales* Geoffrey Chaucer maintained that Lent was the time when people felt most need of both travel and rehabilitation. His characters looked frequently to the weather cock – a traditional form for the weather vanes on church towers – to see which way the wind was blowing and hence the sort of weather that might be expected.

SHINE ON, HARVEST MOON

These words from a popular song of the 1900s celebrate the full moon nearest the autumn equinox, and thus the end of the harvest.

Hanging low on the horizon, the harvest moon appears very large and orange or red, and it is bright enough for the final tasks of the harvest to be completed, if necessary, after sunset.

The harvest moon is usually on display in September but can occur in the early part of October. In American folklore it is also known as the wine moon, the singing moon or the elk call moon. Its colour is explained by the fact that when it is low in the sky its light has to travel further through the atmosphere, which scatters the blue and violet rays but not the reds and oranges. The hunter's moon, which follows it, is almost equally spectacular.

The Tin Pan Alley song 'Shine on, Harvest Moon', by Jack Norworth and his wife Nora Bayes, was first sung in the *Ziegfeld Follies of 1908*:

Oh, shine on, shine on harvest moon
Up in the sky;
I ain't had no lovin'
Since January, April, June or July.
Snow ain't no time to stay
Outdoors and spoon;
So shine on, shine on, harvest moon,
For me and my gal.

The original names of the months in the chorus are often changed to 'January, February, June or July'.

THE MOON BY NAME

The moon of each month is known by one or more names – many of these are Native American designations:

JANUARY – wolf moon, hunger moon

FEBRUARY – snow moon, ice moon

MARCH – worm moon, sap moon, sugaring moon, crow moon, storm moon

APRIL – pink moon, egg moon, grass moon, rain moon, growing moon

MAY – flower moon, planting moon, milk moon, hare moon

JUNE – strawberry moon, rose moon, honey moon, mead moon

JULY – buck moon, thunder moon, deer moon, hay moon

AUGUST – sturgeon moon, corn moon, fruit moon, barley moon

SEPTEMBER – harvest moon

OCTOBER – hunter's moon

NOVEMBER – frosty moon, snow moon, beaver moon

DECEMBER – cold moon, long night moon, winter moon

Year of mushrooms, year of poverty

The reason being that a wet period in late summer, which is conducive to fungal growth, will mar the harvest and severely reduce yields, although it will prove a delight to the lover of wild mushrooms of many kinds.

For most of the year, fungi grow underground, in a hidden mass of threads known as a mycelium, through which they absorb nutrients from decaying organic matter. But in autumn many species push up into the air their array of fruiting bodies, which produce the spores by which they reproduce – a process that depends on both warmth and moisture.

Many of these fruiting bodies, which we call mushrooms or toadstools, are poisonous, but many others are both edible and delicious. Thus it is always wise to take great care over the correct identification of any fungi intended for the table.

The late 18th-century poet James Woodhouse had plenty to say in praise of autumn's fungal harvest and where it can be found:

> *And lovelier far than vernal flow'rs,*
> *Thy mushrooms shooting after show'rs;*
> *That fear no more the fatal scythe,*
> *But proudly bear their bonnets blithe,*
> *With covering form'd of silk and snow,*
> *And lin'd with brightening pink below . . .*
> *Their forms and hues some solace yield,*
> *In wood, or wild, or humid field . . .*

The shadow of poverty caused by a wet season and a poor harvest, with insufficient grain to sell or to feed farm animals, still lingers in rural communities. As recently as 2004, when August saw more than 140 per cent of average rainfall in northern Britain, Yorkshire farmers were salvaging what they could from a pitiful harvest, with crops literally rotting in the fields.

EDIBLE HARVEST

Some of the best autumn mushrooms and how to enjoy them. In her classic *Food in England* of 1954 Dorothy Hartley recommends:

BUTTON MUSHROOMS – stewed in milk with butter, mace and pepper.

HORSE MUSHROOMS – baked with tomatoes and bacon on top.

GIANT PUFFBALL – sliced, dipped in egg and breadcrumbs and fried.

PARASOLS – steamed between two buttered soup plates and eaten with bread and butter.

CHANTERELLES – stewed and served in a creamy white sauce.

BOLETUS (CEPS) – baked in butter.

Beware of false dawns

Metaphorically, an injunction to beware of a promising sign that comes to nothing, based on the faint early morning glow that appears near the horizon around the time of the autumn equinox. Dawn is a time of day that has greatly inspired both writers and artists.

That the darkest hour of the night is just before the dawn is a consoling proverb implying that nothing is all bad and improvement is always possible.

When the sky is very dark, with little light pollution and little or no moonlight, it is possible to see in the eastern sky a glowing light that appears like a cone stretching upwards from the horizon. This is zodiacal light, which is produced by the reflection of sunlight from cosmic dust within the solar system – dust that has lingered in the universe since the solar system came into existence over four billion years ago.

Zodiacal light is so named because it appears to extend from the area from where the sun will soon rise along the ecliptic or zodiac – that is, the line along which the sun will pass as it moves through the heavens. This phenomenon, which was first observed by the Italian astronomer Giovanni Cassini in 1683, can also be seen in spring in the western sky after the sun has set. In addition it may be possible to see an oval glow, known as the *gegenschein*, above the opposite horizon.

A false dawn is easily confused with daybreak. It was chosen by Rudyard Kipling as the title of a short story set around a hill station during

the period of the British Raj, in which an eligible bachelor organizes a moonlit picnic in order to propose marriage to a girl, then realizes he has been too hasty and is actually in love with her sister. Kipling writes: 'The moon was low down, and there was just a glimmer of the false dawn that comes about an hour before the real one. But the light was very faint . . .'

WRITERS' DAWNS

Descriptions of dawn abound in poetry and prose:

'And a grey mist on the sea's face and a
 grey dawn breaking.'
(*Sea Fever*, John Masefield)

'The moon on the one hand, the dawn on
 the other:
The moon is my sister the dawn is my
 brother.'
(*The Early Morning*, Hilaire Belloc)

'Ah, sad and strange as in dark summer
 dawns.'
(*The Princess*, Alfred, Lord Tennyson)

'Say, has some wet bird-haunting
 English lawn
Lent it the music of its trees at dawn?'
 (*Parting*, Matthew Arnold)

CHAPTER 2

FORETELLLING
THE WEATHER

From the ever-changing clouds to the colour of the night sky, there are literally hundreds of signs that have been used over the millennia to forecast the weather. And, not least because of our sceptical view of weather forecasters, many traditional ideas – such as 'Red sky at night, shepherd's delight' – still hold our attention because they contain an element of the truth. Nearly all the sayings included in this chapter apply in the short term – a reflection of the intrinsically unsettled nature of the British climate.

Every aspect of the sky features in the lore of the weather, not least the rainbow, which, after the Biblical flood, was God's sign to Noah. Day to day, however, cloud watching is one of the most compelling pastimes, and cloud spotting has become, for some, almost a compulsion. Signs that the weather is changing can almost invariably be predicted by changes in the clouds. In the mid-19th century, when forecasting was beginning to become more scientific, Admiral Robert Fitzroy made this typical observation: 'After fine, clear weather the first signs in the sky of a coming change are usually light streaks, curls, wisps or mottled patches of white distant clouds, which increase and are followed by an overcasting of murky vapour that grows into cloudiness. The appearance more or less oily or watery, as wind or rain may prevail, is an infallible sign. Usually the higher and more distant such clouds seem to be, the more gradual, but general, the coming change of the weather will be.' Add to these the changes recorded by the barometer and you will quickly become your own weather forecaster.

THE MOON AND THE WEATHER MAY CHANGE TOGETHER

The first line of a verse that continues: 'But the change of the moon does not change the weather'. The cycles of the moon may indeed be related to small changes in the weather, though they do not, as was once thought, control the rain and dew.

Scientists studying the weather around the world have, perhaps surprisingly, discovered that at certain places on the west coasts of Australia and India, and in Jakarta, rainfall is slightly less heavy at the full moon than at other times in the lunar cycle. What is more, accurate measurements from satellites have recorded that, on average, the night-time temperature is 0.02°C higher at full moon, a phenomenon that has yet to be explained and is certainly not due to any warming effect of moonlight.

The way in which we see the moon is affected by its eccentric orbit around the earth: every 18.6 years it comes to a lunar standstill, when it appears at its lowest in the sky. Not only does this pattern coincide with patterns of drought in the western USA, in the past it influenced the building and alignment of megalithic monuments such as the standing stones at Avebury in England and Carnac in France.

The association between rain and the moon is an ancient one, for the moon was once said to control all things moist. It was believed that dew formed because the moon was able to suck up vapours from the earth during the night, allowing them to fall back to the ground at dawn. In an almanac of 1604 Edward Pond explained the thinking of the time (the spelling has been modernized): 'There are four Elements, viz. Fire, Air, Water, and Earth: The Fire is hot and dry, very light, aspiring, bright and clear, placed above the air, next under the orb of the Moon . . . The Air hot and moist, ascending, light and clear, by his heat joined to the fire, and by his moisture joined to the water . . .'

The colour of the moon has also been held to be significant to the weather, as in the rhyme:

Pale moon doth rain, red moon doth blow,
White moon doth neither rain nor snow.

THE NORTH WIND DOTH BLOW AND WE SHALL HAVE SNOW

The first line of a children's verse but also true, because cold wind blowing from the north and meeting warmer, damp, unstable air is a common cause of snowfall.

In full, the rhyme from which this saying originates, which is believed to date from the 16th century, runs:

The North wind doth blow and we shall
have snow,
And what will poor robin do then, poor thing?
He'll sit in a barn and keep himself warm
And hide his head under his wing, poor thing.

Snow forms in clouds that are below freezing, but will only fall as snow – rather than rain – when the temperature is low enough for it to reach the ground without melting. What usually happens is that warm air flows up and over cold air, causing water vapour to supercool into ice crystals. When these become so large that they can no longer be kept aloft by the clouds, they fall as snow.

Storms powerful enough to create blizzards, in which heavy snow is accompanied by winds of 72km/h (45mph) or more, usually form when the polar jet stream is placed so that cold air from the north clashes violently with warm air from the south, often to the northwest of intense storm systems. The effects on humans can be devastating, as Ralph Abercromby described in *Weather* (1887): 'The wind drives the cold into the bones even through fur clothing and raises a blinding dust of powdery snow. If wood cannot be found, nature can only resist the cold for a number of hours, and the men are frozen to death if no shelter can be found.'

MORE SNOW LORE

The first three of these sayings about snow contain more than an element of the truth:

It takes three cloudy days to bring a heavy snow.

When the snow falls dry,
    it means to lie;
But flakes light and soft
    bring rain oft.

When snow falls in the mud, it remains all winter.

The number of days the last snow remains on the ground indicates the number of snowstorms that will occur the following winter.

IF THE SNOWFLAKES INCREASE IN SIZE, A THAW WILL FOLLOW

A generally correct observation, since snowflakes tend to be larger at higher temperatures. It is one of the wonders of nature that no two snowflakes are ever exactly alike.

Between freezing 0°C (32°F) and -3°C (27°F) snow forms thin, flat planar crystals that can regularly be as large as 25mm (1in) in diameter, but between -3°C (27°F) and -8°C (18°F) it forms needles, hollow columns or prisms, which are often smaller. When snowflakes melt and freeze again they form ball-like pellets known as graupel. The biggest snowflakes ever recorded fell in Montana on 28 January 1887 and, according to the *Monthly Weather Review* for that year, measured a massive 38cm (15in) across and 20cm (8in) thick.

The likelihood of snow turning to rain was closely and accurately observed by George F. Chambers, a barrister and one of Britain's leading amateur astronomers, in his *Weather Predictions* of 1877: 'If, after severe cold it begins to snow, and the wind veers from E. to S.E., and the barometer falls and the cold becomes less intense, still the thermometer may remain below 32°. In such a case, when the wind reaches the S., the snow does *not* turn to rain, and if the southerly current is displaced the snow will continue almost or quite uninterruptedly.'

According to an Anglo-Saxon prediction, a quick thaw is followed by a long frost.

Snow crystals have been observed since ancient times. Around 135 BC the Chinese author Han Ying wrote that 'flowers of snow are always six-pointed' and in

1250, in the oldest detailed description of snowflakes, the Dominican friar and bishop Albertus Magnus commented on their star-like nature. Other scientists conducted studies of snowflakes, notably the mathematician Johannes Kepler, who wrote at length in 1611 on snowflakes and their hexagonal nature. The French philosopher René Descartes and the microscopist Robert Hooke also made observations on snow. But it was Wilson Alwyn Bentley, a farmer from Jericho, Vermont – who became known as the 'Snowflake Man' – who created the first photographic catalogue of more than 5,000 snowflakes, made over 40 successive winters; many of these were published in his 1931 book *Snow Crystals*. Ironically, Bentley died that same year, having contracted pneumonia after walking home in a blizzard.

In his poem 'Thaw', Edward Thomas saw the melting snow as a sign of winter's demise:

Over the land freckled with snow half-thawed
The speculating rooks at their nests cawed
And saw from elm-tops, delicate as flower of grass,
What we below could not see, Winter pass.

NORTH WINDS SEND HAIL

They may do, but not necessarily, since this saying is part of a winter prediction. In fact, hail is more often a phenomenon of summer than of winter.

The saying in question comes from the winter prognostications set out in farmer Thomas Tusser's long poem *Five Hundred Points of Good Husbandry*, first published in 1557:

North winds send hail, south winds bring rain.
East winds we bewail, west winds blow amain:

North-east is too cold, south-east not too warm,
North-west is too bold, south-west doth no harm.

In Britain hail in winter is common on the coasts, especially in the north. Here it can fall as small opaque pellets of 'soft hail', formed when a stream of cool air coming from the west (not the north) passes over the land. By contrast with hard hail (see page 147), soft hail is whiter and less dense because it contains air bubbles. Soft hail forms at a temperature below freezing when ice crystals and small, supercooled water and cloud droplets merge.

In the USA, the area where the states of Colorado, Nebraska and Wyoming meet is dubbed 'hail alley' from the frequency of hailstorms there. Cheyenne, Wyoming, is North America's most hail-prone city.

The Dorset poet William Barnes described in his 'Life of Last Year' the effects on the countryside of winter's weather, including hail:

Though now, while the March wind is keen,
The holly and ivy are green,
We ev'rywhere see in our walks,
By hedge or by wood, wither'd stalks;
Some stout that, unholden, have stood;
Some weak that have hung on green wood,
But beaten by rain, and by hail,
And snow, in the winterly gale,
Now totter or quiver all sear,
Dead shapes of the life of last year.

WHEN THE NEW MOON HOLDS THE OLD ONE IN HER LAP, EXPECT FAIR WEATHER

If at new moon the air is very clear, it is possible to see the whole moon as a dim grey ball. Such conditions are most likely to occur during a settled spell of fine weather.

The moon and its phases have long been said by country folk to coincide with weather patterns, although evidence for the truth of these predictions is scant. Such sayings are more likely to have arisen in reverse – as a result of prevailing weather and its effects on the visibility of the moon.

After a new moon, the period when it is waxing towards fullness has long been regarded as a propitious time for all kinds of activities, including sowing seeds, particularly of root crops, pruning and grafting apple trees, shearing sheep and killing food animals such as pigs. It is therefore no coincidence that it is believed that mutton killed when the moon is on the wane will 'shrink in the pot'.

The orientation of the new moon in the sky has also been held to be significant to the weather. A new moon on its back is said to signify wind but no rain, because you can 'hang your hat on its horns'. If the new moon appears to stand on one point it said to forebode rain in summer and snow in winter.

If you wish to be rich it is said that when you first see the new moon you should turn over all the money in your pockets, or take it out and show it to the moon. But you should never point at the new moon – that is the way to bring trouble on you and yours.

The Roman poet Virgil, the son of a farmer and a student of astronomy, was a keen observer of the weather and wrote of the new moon and its appearance (in Dryden's translation):

When the moon first appears, if then she shrouds
Her silver crescent tipped with sable clouds,
Conclude she bodes a tempest on the main,
And brews for fields impetuous floods of rain;
Or if her face with fiery flushings glow,
Expect the rattling winds aloft to blow;
But four nights old (for that's the surest sign)
With sharpened horns, if glorious then she shine,
Next day, nor only that, but all the moon,
Till her revolving race be wholly run,
Are void of tempest both by land and sea.

IF TWO RAINBOWS APPEAR AT ONCE, MORE RAIN IS TO COME

Quite possibly, although rainbows, whether single or double, indicate only the weather conditions at the time at which they appear.

The rainbow, said by the Bible to be the sign from God to Noah that he would never flood the earth again, is created when falling rain is illuminated by sunlight. Each raindrop breaks up the light into the spectrum of colours, but it is also reflected at least once before leaving the drop. A single bow is created by one internal reflection; a secondary bow, outside the primary one and with its colours reversed, is the result of two internal reflections.

The rainbow is an arc of a circle whose centre is always at the same distance below the horizon as the sun's altitude above it, so the higher the sun the lower the top of the bow. For this reason, the best rainbows are to be seen near sunrise or sunset, when it is possible to see the exact spot of the rainbow's end, where a pot of gold is said to be located. Small rainbow-like bright spots sometimes seen alongside the sun near the horizon are known as sun dogs.

MORE RAINBOW PREDICTIONS

Some rainbow forecasts do hold more than a grain of truth:

A rainbow in the morning: sailors take warning.
Because more rain is on the way – a morning rainbow lies in the west, from where wet weather is likely to approach the British Isles.

If the rainbow comes at night, the rain is gone quite.
An evening rainbow is viewed from the east, after rain showers are passing, or have already passed away.

Less reliable are notions such as:

When the rainbow does not reach down to the water, clear weather will follow.

If a blue colour should predominate, the air is clearing.

If the red colour is conspicuous, expect both wind and rain.

Saturday rainbow, a week's rotten weather.

Black spots on the sun indicate rain

Or so it was said by Theophrastus. It now seems that there is some kind of correlation between sunspots and the weather, though not necessarily related to precipitation.

Sunspots are dark areas on the sun that indicate magnetic activity. Their number has been found to rise quickly, then gradually fall back, in a cycle of about 11 years. They were first observed in 1610 by three astronomers, Thomas Harriot of England and Johannes and David Fabricius of Holland.

In 1801 astronomers noted an apparent correlation between wheat prices and solar activity, but it took the advent of weather satellites and modern data analysis to confirm that the link between sunspot activity and the weather does indeed exist. At an 11-year peak, for example, westerly winds often lead to a colder than normal winter in areas such as the southeastern United States. The jet stream sinks southwards, resulting in a cold wet summer in northern Europe. It has also been suggested that the wettest rainy seasons in East Africa in the 20th century were associated with maximum sunspot activity.

Between 1645 and 1715 very few sunspots were observed – about 50 compared with the 40–50,000 seen in a similar period now. This period is known as the Maunder Minimum, named for the astronomer Edward W. Maunder, who analysed it in the 1890s. It coincided with a period of lower than average temperatures worldwide known as the 'Little Ice Age'.

Some say that the dense growth in low temperatures of the wood used to make Stradivarius violins helps to give them their exceptional quality. Antonio Stradivari was born in 1644, the year before the start of the Maunder Minimum.

Wind roaring in chimney, rain to come

This saying links the onset of rain with the increase in wind that accompanies the approach of a depression or cyclone – a passing region of low pressure.

The roaring of wind in a chimney is an effect rather like that of a musical instrument. The wind is funnelled and turned in such a way that sound waves are produced. Wind whirling in the chimney will bring down surplus soot, whose fall is also believed to be a portent of rain.

A long period of rain is announced by a backing wind – that is, a wind that changes direction anti-clockwise – probably from a northerly to a westerly or south-westerly direction, from which, in Britain, the prevailing weather approaches. One way to predict rain from this wind is to stand with your back to it and observe the clouds. If cirrus clouds are spreading to your right, and gradually changing to cirrostratus, then to altostratus, rain is almost certain.

The word 'chimney' comes from the Latin caminus, *meaning a furnace or fireplace. Before the development of the chimney, smoke from a fire would simply leave the hall – the main room of the home – via a hole in the roof.*

From the 12th century until the advent of central heating in the post-war years, the fireplace was the focal point of the living room. Soot falling from the chimney into the fireplace was believed to predict more than the weather, as recorded by the Dorset folklorist J.S. Udal: 'If a piece of soot clings to the bar of the grate it is a sign that a stranger may be expected; and if it hangs down a long flake you can ascertain what day the stranger will come by clapping your hands close to it until it falls off by reason of the current of air thus created, whilst repeating at each stroke the day of the week.'

Dew on the Grass After a Fair Day is the Sign of Another

A relatively accurate forecast, since dew forms during spells of fine weather. Another variation is 'Dew before midnight, tomorrow will be bright'.

Dew tends to form most readily when the air is moist but the sky is clear and there is little wind. Its formation depends, critically, on the temperatures of the air and the ground, and the amount of moisture in the air and the ground. Also crucial is the dew point, the temperature at which the air, when cooled, will become saturated with water vapour. So if on an early autumn evening the dew point is, say, 8°C (48°F) and the ground is still a warm 12°C (54°F) no dew will form. But if the temperature drops to 7°C (45°F) the moisture in the air will begin to condense, forming drops of dew.

The formation of dew was first explained by Dr William Charles Wells in his 1814 *Essay on Dew*, based on meticulous recordings of temperatures of grass and dew formation. Among his many observations was the fact that 'grass, after having been dewed in the evening, is never found dry until after sunrise, unless the weather has, in the meantime, changed.' Following up on these findings, Revd Leonard Jenyns, an amateur meteorologist, deduced that on a clear, calm evening the temperature of the dew point is a fair guide to the minimum temperature that may be expected before sunrise the following day.

These lines from *The Weather Eye* by C.R. Benstead (1940) aptly describe the delights of a dewy morning:

'Tis sweet to hear the songs of birds arise
At early dawn – to gaze on cloudless skies –
To scatter round you, as you lightly pass,
A shower of diamonds from each blade of grass.

WHEN THE MIST COMES FROM THE SEA, GOOD WEATHER WILL IT BE

This is very often true, particularly if the mist is accompanied by a sea breeze and when it forms in the spring and early summer, before the sea has started to warm up.

Sea mist – also known as a sea fret, a sea roke or, in Scotland, a haar – forms when a pocket of warm air passes over cold sea. The air at the bottom of the pocket is cooled by the cold air below it, releasing some of the water within it as condensation, which, in turn, generates mist. If the land is warm the mist will quickly disperse as the fog evaporates, and if the sky above is clear the sun will burn it off and soon emerge. If, however, the sky above is cloudy, then the sea mist may linger all day.

The areas of Britain most affected by sea mist are those along the east coast, especially when the wind is blowing from the east, but they can also occur along the south and southwest coasts. In Lincolnshire sea mist is commonly dubbed 'tide weather', but in fact it bears little relation to the movement of water, except where low tide, as in the Essex estuaries, exposes large areas of sand that warm up relatively quickly. Around the fjords of northern Norway and in Greenland, Arctic sea smoke forms when very cold air flows from the land to the sea.

There is a certain beauty in a sea mist, as evoked by John Masefield in his poem 'Sea Fever', which begins:

> I must go down to the seas again, to the lonely sea and the sky,
> And all I ask is a tall ship and a star to steer her by,
> And the wheel's kick and the wind's song and the white sail's shaking
> And a grey mist on the sea's face, and a grey dawn breaking.

In contrast, the dangers of sea mist are among the hazards Rudyard Kipling includes in his poem 'Who Hath Desired the Sea':

> Who hath desired the Sea? Her menaces swift as her mercies?
> The in-rolling walls of the fog and the silver-winged breeze that disperses?
> The unstable mined berg going South and the calvings and groans that
>   declare it –
> White water half-guessed overside and the moon breaking timely
>   to bare it –
> His Sea as his fathers have dared – his Sea as his children shall dare it:
>   His Sea as she serves him or kills?
> So and no otherwise – so and no otherwise – hillmen desire their Hills.

Goat's hair clouds forebode wind

An accurate saying because goat's hair is a type of cirrus cloud that very often precedes the arrival of both wind and bad weather.

To all but the most avid and observant cloud spotter, goat's hair cloud is very similar to mares' tails (see page 14) but with shorter wisps. In *Weather*, his ground-breaking book of 1887 subtitled 'A Popular Exposition of the Nature of Weather Changes from Day to Day', Ralph Abercromby classifies goat's hair as 'a short bundle of white cirrus hairs and a forerunner of bad weather in every country'. Goat's hair clouds form at very high altitudes at a temperature of around -40°C (-40°F), and are produced most readily when a warm or occluded front is approaching. They are very high in the sky, within the troposphere – the wisps are made of minute ice crystals falling through the air, which are blown sideways by the wind into their characteristic shapes. When these clouds thicken they are transformed into

> The hair-like strand's of goat's hair cloud are also known as 'fallstreaks' and have been aptly described as 'celestial brush strokes'.

nimbostratus, which almost inevitably mean rain or snow. The Roman poet and philosopher Lucretius described this phenomenon in *De rerum natura* ('On the nature of things'), translated by Thomas Creech in 1682:

> *Now clouds combine, and spread o'er all the sky,*
> *When little rugged parts ascend on high,*
> *Which may be twined, though by a feeble tie;*

These make small clouds, which, driven on by wind,
To other like and little clouds are joined,
And these increase by more: at last they form
Thick, heavy clouds; and thence proceeds a storm.

WHEN DUST FLIES IN EDDIES, EXPECT RAIN

Quite possibly a sign of rain, which is associated with a rising wind – large gusts regularly accompany the development of cold fronts and the arrival of precipitation from the south or south-west.

Unlike tornadoes, which descend to the ground from the clouds, dust devils are created by warm air rising from hot, parched ground. The ascending air whirls around, corkscrewing into an ever tighter vortex, reaching speeds of 160km/h (100mph) and sucking up objects in its path – chairs, tables and anything not secured to the ground. As it rises the dust devil sucks in cool air, which dissipates the effect of the vortex, and in seconds the eddy collapses.

Rare in Britain, dust devils are common in desert areas such as the Sahara and the deserts of the southern United States. The Navajo call them *chindi*, and believe that they are the ghosts or spirits of the dead. If the devil spins clockwise it is believed to be a good spirit; if anti-clockwise, a bad one. In Australia they are known as 'whirly-whirlies' and in Aboriginal myth they represent spirit forms. If children misbehave they are often told by their parents that the whirly-whirly will come to take them away.

Dust from the Sahara is commonly blown north to Britain and deposited as a fine film of red dust washed down by rain.

Sound travelling far and wide a stormy day will betide

A phenomenon observed in many different times and places, regarding the sound of everything from the notes of a violin to the hammering of the blacksmith or the sound of an approaching train.

The science behind this saying is that when air is laden with moisture – as before a storm – it conducts sound much better than when it is dry. This is more likely to be true in summer than in winter, because cold air is very dense, which makes it an excellent conductor of sound, but it is also likely to be dry, so in these circumstances sound will not carry over such a long distance.

The subtleties of sound transmission are monitored carefully by country folk. As Richard Inwards says in *Weather Lore* (1898): 'When the people of Monzie [Perthshire] hear the sound of the waterfalls of Shaggie or the roar of the distant Turret clearly and loudly, a storm is expected; but if the sound seems to recede from the ear till it is lost in the distance, and if the weather is thick, a change to fair may be looked for speedily.'

Wind may also have an effect on sounds, as Sir Arthur Mitchell says in his 1860 essay *On the Popular Weather Prognostics of Scotland*: 'In the collieries about Dysart [in Fife], and in some others, it is thought by the miners that before a storm of wind a sound not unlike that of a bagpipe or the buzz of the bee comes from the mineral . . .'

THREE SOUTH-WESTERS THEN ONE HEAVY RAIN

In the British Isles, south-westerly winds are linked with the arrival of rain, often heavy and prolonged, for as the saying goes, 'long foretold, long last'. For millennia the winds have held strong mythological associations.

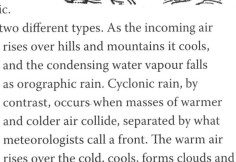

South-westerly winds bring rain to Britain because they hold in them air that is full of water from the Atlantic. However, the rain they herald is of two different types. As the incoming air rises over hills and mountains it cools, and the condensing water vapour falls as orographic rain. Cyclonic rain, by contrast, occurs when masses of warmer and colder air collide, separated by what meteorologists call a front. The warm air rises over the cold, cools, forms clouds and deposits its rain in a steady stream that can last for a few hours or even longer.

A sou'wester is a type of waterproof hat favoured by fishermen. It has a wide brim at the back that is turned down over the neck.

For Shakespeare the south-west wind was not to be welcomed, as portrayed in this exchange between Caliban and Prospero in *The Tempest*:

> CALIBAN: *As wicked dew as e'er my mother brush'd*
> *With raven's feather from unwholesome fen*
> *Drop on you both! A south-west blow on ye*
> *And blister you all o'er!*

> PROSPERO: *For this, be sure, tonight thou shalt have cramps*
> *Side stitches that shall pen thy breath up; urchins*
> *Shall, for that vast of night that they may work,*
> *All exercise on thee . . .*

In Greek mythology, Aeolus was the king of the winds, and kept them locked behind brass doors, releasing them to do their damage only at his command. He could also use them benignly, as when he assisted Odysseus in overcoming sea storms, and as a result he was accorded particular regard by sailors. In the Iroquois tradition, Ga-oh, the benevolent spirit of the winds, lives in the northern sky from where he controls the four winds and also the seasons and human welfare.

IF THERE BE A RAINBOW IN THE EVE IT WILL RAIN AND LEAVE

A weather forecast that is more than likely to be accurate, but is by no means infallible. The colours of the rainbow, once a mystery, were scientifically explained by Isaac Newton.

In the evening, the sun is in the west. If you see a rainbow, which will be visible only if the sun is behind you, it will be in the east. However, if there is enough sunshine to create a bow then it is more than likely that the weather is clearing from west to east and that any rain is on its way out.

Aristotle thought that rainbows were caused by the reflection of sunlight in the clouds, and the rainbow was not properly explained until 1666 when, following his discovery that a prism would break white light into the colours of the spectrum, Isaac Newton put forward his 'geometrical theory'. In a rainbow, some of the light that enters each water drop is reflected at the inner surface of the far side of the drop and the refracted rays leave the drop at different angles, depending on their colour. As a rule, the bigger the raindrops the more intense the colours of the rainbow become. When the drops are small the colours tend to overlap and become less distinct. If there is a gap in the rainbow it is because there is no rain falling there or it is in the shadow of a cloud.

Faintest of all are the colours of a 'moon bow', which appears almost white. Visible on bright moonlit nights, particularly at waterfalls such as Victoria Falls, it is at once ghostly and extraordinary.

RAINBOW SUPERSTITIONS

A rainbow can bring good luck or bad, but on seeing one there are several ways of protecting yourself:

A rainbow that forms over a house is a sign of death.

If you ever see a triple rainbow you will have luck and riches later in life.

To eliminate bad luck, 'cross out' any rainbow you see by making a cross on the ground with twigs or pieces of straw.

Never point at a rainbow or you will have bad luck.

Chant a rhyme such as 'Rainbow, rainbow, bring me luck/If you don't I'll break you up.'

When you see a rainbow, make a wish – it may come true.

SPRINGS RISE AGAINST RAIN

A well-documented phenomenon associated with a fall in pressure, as is the escape of gases from rocks. As well as being the source of health-giving, mineral-rich water, springs and wells have long been believed to have magical or holy properties.

When air pressure drops, as it generally does when rain is on the way, it has the effect of releasing water and gases from under ground. The result is that a spring that appears to have dried up will suddenly gush with water, a phenomenon known as 'earth sweat'. Similarly, a fall in atmospheric pressure has long been identified by underground workers with foul air escaping from crevices in rocks. If the change in the weather is likely to be extreme, miners have reported an accompanying 'sound like the buzzing of insects'.

   A similar effect occurs as rivers rise before rain and, at the shore, bubbles rise up from clam beds. In the countryside, 'ungrateful odours' may be expelled from areas of mud and rotting vegetation when rain is on the way. Or, put more poetically:

> *When ditch and pond offend the nose,*
> *Then look for rain and stormy blows.*

Natural springs, and the wells built at such sites to ease the collection of water, have long been venerated for more than their usefulness. Sadler's Wells in London, for example, was originally known as Holy Well

Pliny maintained in his *Natural History* that before an earthquake: 'Water in wells is muddier and smells foul.'

and its waters were famed for their curative powers. The water of Silver Well, near Otterburn in Northumberland, was believed to be able to convert any object into gold or other precious metal, but only if it received offerings of pine cones. Other offerings made to wells have included pottery (ideally smashed) and even human skulls. Tossing a coin into a wishing well is a way of ensuring good fortune.

THE HIGHER THE CLOUDS THE FAIRER THE WEATHER

Sometimes true, sometimes not: some 'fair weather' clouds form at much lower levels than some rain-bearing types. In fine weather extraordinary cloud formations can be seen.

The most common of fair weather clouds are the cotton-wool puffs of cumulus that float across the sky on a sunny day. These clouds, which are about 1.6km (1 mile) above the ground, are created on thermals – columns of warmed air rising from the ground. As the air gets warmer during the day these clouds tend to evaporate and disappear altogether. The highest of all clouds, the cirrus, at up to 13km (8 miles) from the ground, may eventually develop into rain clouds, but when thin and streaky will certainly not be harbingers of rain.

The different types of cumulus cloud are among those that form the shapes and patterns in the sky so beloved of cloud watchers. In *Antony and Cleopatra* Shakespeare expresses their fascination:

In fine weather, aircraft vapour trails produce streaks of manmade cloud that can spread out for thousands of square kilometres and, as they do so, trigger the formation of thin cirriform cloud.

Sometimes we see a cloud that's dragonish;
A vapour sometime like a bear or lion,
A tower'd citadel, a pendant rock,
A forked mountain, or blue promontory
With trees upon't, that nod unto the world,
And mock our eyes with air.

FAIR WEATHER CLOUDS

Cumulus clouds come in a variety of forms, some of which can indeed produce rain:

CUMULUS HUMILIS – the smallest and shallowest – look wide and flat.

CUMULUS MEDIOCRIS – larger and taller, possibly with fluffy 'sproutings' on top.

CUMULUS RADIATUS – form rows or 'cloud streets' more or less parallel to the direction of the wind.

CUMULUS FRACTUS – have ragged edges and a fractured look; these can sometimes form underneath rain clouds.

CUMULUS CONGESTUS – the tallest of the cumulus clouds, and capable of producing short, sharp showers.

The Deeper the Cloud the Harder it Showers

A reliable forecast based on the close association between heavy rainfall and the appearance of towering cumulonimbus clouds. Large clouds that decrease in size are, by contrast, predictors of fair weather.

Cumulus clouds are heaped but cumulonimbus are towering, mountainous structures, named from the Latin *nimbus* meaning 'rain'. The base of each cloud is usually dark and the top is either wispy and fibrous, where water is freezing into ice crystals, or flattened into an anvil shape. From clouds such as this, heavy 'hard' showers may easily develop into full-scale thunderstorms.

> It is said by sailors that when cumulus clouds become heaped up to leeward during a strong wind at sunset thunder may be expected during the night.

Cumulonimbus clouds are created when the air is deeply unstable, mostly in summer when upward air currents are strongest. These clouds form quickly and are usually short-lived. Once they have dropped their payload of rain – or hail or even snow – they may quickly peter out.

If pendulous breast-like blobs of cloud hang from the underside of the anvil (a formation described as cumulonimbus with mammatus) then a severe thunderstorm is imminent – and possibly even a tornado.

A cumulonimbus cloud with an anvil top is known as a cumulonimbus incus. The largest of these, which are especially common in the tropics, can reach 10km (6 miles) in height – taller than Mount Everest. Ahead of a very severe storm you may see the anvil bulge. This is caused by an updraught of air carrying a parcel of cloud into the stratosphere.

Red sky at night, shepherd's delight; red sky in the morning, shepherd's warning

Wherever the weather comes predominantly from the west, the first part of this saying is one of the most reliable weather forecasts.

Colours in the sky arise from dust and moisture in the atmosphere splitting and scattering the sun's light. At the beginning and end of each day, when sunlight travels farthest through the atmosphere to reach the earth, the 'long' red, orange and yellow rays of the spectrum are scattered least, and are therefore most visible. If, as the sun sets, the sky glows a rosy pink, this signals dry air in the west, from where the next day's weather will arrive. A more livid sky predicts the opposite.

In the morning, a yellow sky also forecasts rain. If it is red the chance of rain depends on the type and extent of the clouds. As the 19th-century weather forecaster C.L. Prince observed: 'If at sunrise small reddish-looking clouds are seen low on the horizon, it must not always be considered to indicate rain . . . It has frequently been observed that if [the clouds] extend ten degrees, rain will follow before two or three pm; but if still higher and nearer the zenith [the point directly above the observer], rain will fall within three hours.'

It is thought that this is one of the oldest of weather sayings, and it is likely to have been passed on by word of mouth before it was ever written down. There is a written version in Matthew XVI in the Wyclif Bible, from as early as

1395, which in its modern translation reads: 'When it is evening, ye say, It will be fair weather: for the sky is red. And in the morning, It will be foul weather to day: for the sky is red and louring.' In *Venus and Adonis*, written in 1593, Shakespeare puts it even more poetically:

Like a red morn, that ever yet betokened
Wreck to the seaman, tempest to the field,
Sorrow to shepherds, woe unto the birds,
Gust and foul flaws to herdmen and to herds.

RAIN TO COME?

Some other weather sayings for the beginning and end of the day:

Cloudy mornings turn to clear evenings.

At sunset with a cloud so black,
A westerly wind you shall not lack.

Rain is sure to follow after frost that melts before the sun rises.

If the weather changes at night, it will not last when the day breaks.

Three foggy mornings indicate rain.

If it rains when the sun shines it will rain next day.

If the sun in red should set, the next day surely will be wet

This saying makes the opposite prediction to the well-known 'red sky at night', but it is equally valid in different circumstances, particularly when the wind is in the east.

Moisture in the atmosphere, whether in the evening or the morning, makes the light disperse in such a way that it creates the vivid yellow or reddish-orange clouds that predict rain. To the observant eye these look quite different from the benign pink sky that heralds a fine dawn.

> *A grey sky at night, with thick cloud, can indicate an approaching depression. But a thin grey mist in the morning will often disperse to give a fine day.*

Interpreting the colours of the sky has long preoccupied weather observers. Francis Bacon, writing in the 1620s, says: 'If the rays of the sun on rising are not yellow, but ruddy, it denotes rain rather than wind. The same likewise holds good of the setting.'

Studying the sky of the Mediterranean region, the poet Virgil expressed his reliable sunset predictions thus (in Dryden's translation):

> *But more than all the setting sun survey,*
> *When down the steep of heav'n he drives the day;*
> *For oft we find him finishing his race,*
> *With various colours erring on his face.*

If fiery red his glowing globe descends,
High winds and furious tempests he portends;
But, if his cheeks are swoln with livid blue,
He bodes wet weather by his wat'ry hue;
If dusky spots are varied on his brow,
And streaked with red, a troubled colour show,
That sullen mixture shall at once declare
Winds, rain and storms, and elemental war.

RAIN BEFORE SEVEN, FINE BY ELEVEN

An old English saying, and a good forecast in many temperate locations, as long as you are liberal enough to take 'seven' and 'eleven' to mean early and late morning.

This saying works because the weather that accompanies a depression is unlikely to last more than four to eight hours, and rainfall that began the previous evening is likely to peter out before noon. A depression or low pressure area is formed when masses of cold and warm air meet: the warm air rises over the cold, clouds develop and rain falls. If the pressure drops even more it becomes windy as air is sucked in because, as in the old schoolroom rhyme, 'Winds always blow from high to low [pressure].'

Rain, technically 'precipitation that reaches the ground in liquid form', results from droplets colliding and combining

On average, a raindrop measures 2mm ($^1/_{12}$in) in diameter.

inside a turbulent cloud until they are large enough to fall. Alternatively, when supercooled water droplets and ice crystals co-exist in a cloud, water droplets move towards and enlarge the ice crystals until they are large enough to fall as rain, sleet or snow, depending on the temperature.

> *The contrary saying, 'Fine before seven, rain by eleven,' is one that is not to be relied on, although it is often true that 'A cloudy morning bodes a fair afternoon.'*

LONG FORETOLD, LONG LAST; SHORT NOTICE, SOON PASSED

Another reliable forecast, because when the barometer rises or falls slowly and steadily a long spell of fine or foul weather usually follows. Equally, if the glass rises or falls rapidly the weather that follows is not likely to last long.

The Shepherd of Banbury incorporated this prediction into the 14th of his 25 weather rules, which appeared in 1670: 'Sudden rains never last long; but when the air grows thick by degrees, and the sun, moon and stars shine dimmer and dimmer, then it is likely to rain six hours usually.' The later 'interpretation' of the rules published in 1744 underlines the accuracy of this observation and adds many other signs that 'give us previous Notice of rainy weather', including 'the Trefoil [that] swells in the stalk . . . so that it stands up very stiff, but the Leaves droop and hang down', and the 'sweating' of stones and swelling of wood.

The rain produced in these two circumstances is named according to the way in which it comes about. Long-lasting cyclonic rain is caused when moist air is raised by a wedge of cold air pushing underneath it. As a result stratiform clouds increase, the wind backs and the barometer falls. By contrast, convection rain is essentially no more than a passing shower and gets its name from its association with convection currents in the atmosphere, created by warm air rising from the ground.

The barometer was the invention of the Italian physicist Evangelista Torricelli, who in 1643 put a glass tube 1.2m (4ft) long, filled with mercury and sealed at one end, into a bowl of mercury and found that some of the mercury, supported by pressure in the atmosphere, remained within the tube. He also discovered that the level rose in fine weather and dropped when it rained. It was another 150 years before the Frenchman Jean Nicolas Fortin produced an accurate version of Torricelli's design; the disc-shaped aneroid barometer with a needle pointer was invented by another Frenchman, Lucien Vidie, in 1843.

SHORT AND SHARP

Weather lore has plenty to say about showers and their duration:

A sunshiny shower
Never lasts half an hour.

Bright rain makes fools fain [glad].

Sunshine and shower, rain again tomorrow.

Small rain abates high wind.

If short showers come during dry weather they will 'harden' a drought.

The faster the rain, the quicker the hold up.

Ring round the moon, snow soon

In winter, quite possibly. Or the ring could be a sign that rain is on the way, depending on how cold it is. But it needs to be the right kind of ring.

On a winter's night, a pale ring or halo around the moon – shimmering with faint rainbow colours, with the red on the inside – is a magnificent sight, often more spectacular because many of the stars are blotted out by cloud. Sometimes the effect lasts for only a few minutes, but if it persists for longer you may see the different colours strengthen and fade as the ice crystals causing the ring move about, turning and swirling in the cloud.

The moon's halo is created by millions of minute, hexagonal ice crystals, often borne on moisture-laden cirrostratus cloud. In its infancy, the cloud is thin and high enough – about 6,000m (22,000ft) above the ground – to be penetrated by the sun's rays illuminating the moon from below the horizon. The halo appears because each of the ice crystals bends the sun's light twice. If the cloud then thickens and lowers, snow or rain will almost certainly fall. If the cloud disperses then it won't.

A similar phenomenon, the corona, appears as a brownish ring with bluish-white colours towards the inside. If red is there at all it will be to the outside. Because it is formed by sunlight passing through a general dispersal of water droplets in the atmosphere, not ice

Less reliably, sailors also believe that a new moon on a Saturday or a full moon on a Sunday foretell bad weather. The combination occurring in succession is considered to be the worst of both worlds.

in clouds, a corona round the moon can also be a predictor of the weather, though not necessarily a reliable one.

Seamen have long looked to the moon for signs of the weather to come, like the old sailor in Henry Wadsworth Longfellow's poem 'The Wreck of the Hesperus':

> *'I pray thee, put into yonder port,*
> *For I fear a hurricane.*
> *Last night the moon had a golden ring,*
> *And to-night no moon we see.'*

Farmers also take note of the moon, as in the rhyme:

> *If the moon show a silver shield,*
> *Be not afraid to reap your field;*
> *But if she rises haloed round,*
> *Soon we'll tread on deluged ground.*

CHAPTER 3

AROUND
THE YEAR

Year by year, the progression of the months and seasons brings changes in the weather. In the words of the old rhyme attributed to the writer and clergyman Sydney Smith (1771–1845): 'Spring: slippy, drippy, nippy. Summer: showery, flowery, bowery. Autumn: hoppy, croppy, poppy. Winter: wheezy, sneezy, breezy.' Although spring, summer, autumn and winter 'officially' begin in March, June, September and December, it is the weather and the temperature, not the date on the calendar, that actually determines our attitude on a daily basis. The British weather can change so quickly that we can, for instance, be fooled into thinking that spring has arrived on a mild February day, only to find snow falling a day or two later.

Many seasonal weather predictions attempt to forecast one season from another, as in 'Winter finds out what summer lays up' and 'Much fog in autumn, much snow in winter'. Sayings of this kind are in fact notoriously unreliable, but a few are included here for interest. Every month of the year also has its own collection of weather sayings – some, as ever, more believable than others. Many, as one might expect, relate closely to the rhythm of the farming year, on which livelihoods and survival still depend, and to the tasks of the gardener. As with the seasons, the sages of old did their best to forecast future weather from the events of any particular month, as in 'A wet June makes a dry September' and 'When the months of July, August and September are unusually hot, January will be the coldest month'. These we can also take with a pinch of salt – yet keep up our own records to discover the patterns of the weather.

A January spring is worth nothing

Not least because warm weather too early in the year can prompt plants and crops to start into growth prematurely, only to be damaged or even killed by frosts. The January weather is believed by many to predict what is to come later in the year.

Although it has been dubbed the 'blackest month in all the year', a cold January is much more to be welcomed than a warm one. As W.S. Mansfield points out in *The Farmer's Friend* of 1947, 'Cold, dry, frosty weather at this time of year will do a minimum of harm and a maximum of good.' As gardeners will recognize, January frost is beneficial in breaking up the soil to a fine tilth, ideal for sowing seeds and setting out young plants later in the year.

In Spain it is said that the month of January is like a gentlemen because 'as he begins, so he goes on'.

Predictions for the year, based on what January brings, have a long history, and involve elements of superstition as well as the weather itself. Typical is this doom-laden prognostication in the *Almanac of Erra Pater*, reputedly the predictions of a learned Jewish philosopher, published in English by the 17th-century astrologer William Lilly (here with the spelling modernized): 'If the year that January shall enter on a Sunday, that winter shall be cold and moist, the Summer shall be hot, and the time of Harvest shall be windy and rainy, with great abundance of corn, of wines, and other grains, & of all garden fruits, & herbs, there shall be little Oil, abundance shall be of all manner of flesh, some great news shall men hear spoken of Kings and Prelates of the Church, and also of great Princes, great wars and robberies shall be made, and many young people shall die.'

As the days lengthen the cold strengthens

A correct conclusion, because, in northern latitudes, the sea continues to cool down after the winter solstice on 21 December. But the lowest temperatures do not necessarily occur on 14 January, the date midway between the end of autumn and the beginning of spring.

Because the sea cools more slowly than the land, British weather generally continues to get colder throughout January and February. This means that when cold air blows from the north – especially when high pressure systems bring Arctic winds south – there is nothing to temper their effects. Occasionally, however, 'old wives' summers' – periods of unseasonably warm weather – occur in December and January, tempting frogs to spawn well before Christmas.

The winter solstice is St Thomas's Day, when it is said that at noon you should see which way the wind is blowing. Whatever the direction, it will stay the same for the next lunar quarter.

On the shortest day the sun rises least high in the sky and rises and sets at its most southerly points on the northern hemisphere horizon. This is because the earth tilts at 23.4° to its orbit around the sun. In winter the tilt is away from the sun, in the summer towards it.

Frost on the shortest day is considered by some to be an omen of

a severe winter to come, though this is not borne out by statistics. However, in 1564, John Stow recorded: 'The 21. of December began a Frost, which continued so extreamely that on New-yeares even people went over and along the Thamis on the Ice from London-bridge to Westminster, some played at foote-ball as boldly there, as if it had been on dry land.'

FEBRUARY FILL THE DYKE, WEATHER EITHER BLACK OR WHITE

February is a month that can be wet and cold, often with frost and snow. However, rain at this time of year is welcome in the countryside, to fill the dykes and reservoirs and to ensure plentiful supplies for the year to come.

A dry February is certainly not to be welcomed, for as the old verse runs:

> *If in February there be no rain,*
> *They hay won't goody, nor the grain.*
> *All other months of the year*
> *Most heartily curse a fine Februeer.*

The weather in February is fickle indeed, but it is a month of promise, heralded by the flowering of snowdrops, the 'fair maids of February'. Trees such as the weeping willow are just beginning to bud and catkins of hazel and 'pussy willow' decorate lanes and hedges.

The month gets its name from the Latin *februum*, meaning 'purgation', as in the Roman era this was traditionally a time of ritual purification. For Christians it sees the start of the season of Lent. In the Roman calendar, February was the only month with an even number of days, odd numbers being considered more propitious; only in leap years does it have 29 days.

FEBRUARY WEATHER

Letter writers and keepers of diaries comment regularly on February weather, bad and good, as these extracts quoted in Mrs Head's 1917 *Weather Calendar* testify:

4 February 1597
The 4 of February, and in the night following, fell such an abundance of snow, that on the fifth morning, the same was found at London to lye two foote deep in the shallowest. (John Stow)

19 February 1798
I walked to Stowey before dinner . . . returned alone. A fine, sunny, clear, frosty day. The sea still, and blue, and broad, and smooth.
(Dorothy Wordsworth)

21 February 1818
The Thrushes and Blackbirds have been singing me into an idea that it was Spring, and almost that leaves were on the trees. So that black clouds and boisterous winds seem to have mustered and collected in full Divan, for the purpose of convincing me to the contrary. (John Keats)

26 February 1768
We are drowning again for the second winter, and hear of nothing but floods and desolation. (Horace Walpole)

So many mists in March, so many frosts in May

A saying from the 17th century that, although it does not hold completely true, has a germ of truth in it. Frosts in May are something of which gardeners, in particular, need to be acutely aware.

The meteorological link between March mist and May frost is high pressure. In spring so-called radiation fog forms on clear, still nights, when the ground loses heat by radiation and cools the adjoining air to saturation point. In similar conditions in May, cool air condenses on the ground as frost. However, over a period of 25 years, measurements of the weather in Lyneham and Boscombe Down in Wiltshire, the county where this saying is believed to have originated, has proved it to be untrue – as have readings taken at seven other weather stations around Britain.

The portents of mist, a suspension of small droplets in the air, are interpreted differently depending on its position, as in the old Scottish proverb:

> *When the mist taks to the hill*
> *Then gude weather it doth spill:*
> *When the mist taks to the sea*
> *Then gude weather it will be.*

Writing of May frosts in his *Country Calendar* of 1935, the English farmer, writer and broadcaster A.G. Street says: 'She [May] brought winter back to the countryside. Both frost and cold east wind she has used to put a brake on Spring, and in all her temper she does not seem to be woman enough to weep. Still, the countryside need not worry very much over her icy mood, for two reasons. Firstly, because her chilliness is unseasonable, and cannot last, for June will soon be here; and secondly, because the first four months of the year gave everything such a good start that the countryside can withstand May's cold with equanimity.'

> Gardeners are well aware of the damage that late frosts can do, and the wise will not put out tender annuals and bedding plants until the risk has passed. Luckily for modern horticulturalists, aids such as cloches, polytunnels and horticultural fleece are widely available to keep plants protected against frost.

ON THE FIRST OF MARCH, CROWS BEGIN TO SEARCH

Probably a reference to the liking that crows have for eating the eggs of other birds, which are laid at around this time. The behaviour of these little-loved birds, which have long been symbols of evil, is also alleged to forecast the weather.

Britain is home to two species of crow. Most common is the all-black carrion crow (*Corvus corone*). The hooded crow (*C. cornix*), which has black and grey plumage and a black head, breeds mainly in Scotland. All types of crow are particularly unloved by sheep farmers, since they will harass pregnant ewes and attack newborn lambs. The hooded crow got the name

'Royston crow' from its habit of travelling south in winter to haunt the downs in that area of Hertfordshire in order to feed on the carcasses of any casualties among the many sheep grazing there.

Crows have long been considered to be the embodiment of witches, spying on frail mortals and molesting their chosen victims. Single crows were – and are still by some – believed to be the most dangerous. A crow that landed on a house was regarded as a sign of death and even seeing a crow was deemed unlucky. To deter evil it was necessary to say a word such as 'break' or to threaten it with a rhyme such as this one from the north of England:

Crow, crow, get out of my sight,
Or else I'll eat thy liver and thy lights.

THE WEATHER ACCORDING TO CROWS

Crow actions that may – or may not – predict the weather:

'When crows go to the water, if they beat it with their wings, throw it over them, and scream, it foreshadows storms.' (Francis Bacon, 1561–1626)

'If the crow hath any interruption in her note like *hiccough* or croak with a kind of swallowing, it signifies wind and rain.' (John Worlidge, 1640–1700)

'The crow if it caw thrice immediately after daybreak, indicates fair weather, but crying in fine weather indicates a storm.' (Theophrastus c. 371–287 BC)

'The crow with clam'rous cries the
     shower demands,
And single stalks along the desert sands.'
(Virgil 70–19 BC)

March comes in like a lion and goes out like a lamb

Or vice versa. Another popular saying reflecting changeable spring weather is 'In beginning or in end/March its gifts will send.' And March is a month that has provoked much comment from poets and naturalists alike.

Hailing the first good weather in March, William Wordsworth wrote in a poem addressed to his sister Dorothy:

It is the first mild day of March:
Each minute sweeter than before . . .
There is a blessing in the air
Which seems a sense of joy to yield
To the bare trees, and mountains bare.

March is the time when the natural world begins to come to life again, and the weather is important to its progress. As the botanist L.J.F. Brimble commented in *The Floral Year* (1949): 'March should be dry and neither too warm or too cold. But we cannot depend on this, and it is a matter of grave concern, because the plants are beginning to stir themselves, the buds on the trees are bursting, and so all the tender tissues are exposed, and these are very sensitive to temperature.' As to the botanical riches of the countryside, he goes on to warn that '. . . so far as making discoveries are concerned this must be regarded as possibly a month of bitter disappointments or one of pleasant surprises.'

The March sun causes dust, and the winds blow it about

March is noted not only for its windiness but also for its general unpredictability. It is welcomed as the start of spring, and the season for predicting the summer weather to come.

Dust in March is the result of a spell of dry weather, often welcome after the cold and wet of February, although in Wiltshire it is said that it is 'better to be bitten by a snake than to feel the sun in March'. However, in most weather lore the wind is much more welcome, as is the dust it creates, according to the couplet: 'A bushel of March dust is a thing/Worth the ransom of a king.'

William Morris, the 19th-century designer, writer and lover of nature, summed up the qualities of March in his long poem *The Earthly Paradise*:

> *Slayer of the winter, art thou here again?*
> *O welcome, thou that bring'st the summer nigh!*
> *The bitter wind makes not thy victory vain,*
> *Nor will we mock thee for thy faint blue sky.*
> *Welcome, O March! Whose kindly days and dry*
> *Make April ready for the throstle's song,*
> *Thou first redresser of the winter's wrong!*

The month of March is named from Mars, the Roman god of war, but to the Anglo-Saxons it was *hlyd-monat*, meaning 'loud and strong'. They also called it *lencten-monat* or lengthening month, taking note of the significant increase in daylight hours leading up to the equinox (hence the English name 'Lent' for the liturgical period before Easter).

APRIL SHOWERS BRING FORTH MAY FLOWERS

A fitting tribute to the changeable weather typical of early spring, which can be plagued by wintry conditions or wreathed in sunshine. This is a time of year much praised by poets.

The spring weather, and the floral bounty of the season, was famously celebrated by Robert Browning in his poem 'Home Thoughts from Abroad':

Oh, to be in England
Now that April's there,
And whoever wakes in England
Sees, some morning, unaware,
That the lowest boughs and the brushwood sheaf
Round the elm-tree bole are in tiny leaf,
While the chaffinch sings on the orchard bough
In England – now!

And after April, when May follows,
And the whitethroat builds, and all the swallows
Hark! where my blossomed pear-tree in the hedge
Leans to the field and scatters on the clover
Blossoms and dewdrops – at the bent spray's edge –
That's the wise thrush; he sings each song twice over,
Lest you should think he never could recapture
The first fine careless rapture!

And though the fields look rough with hoary dew,
All will be gay when noontide wakes anew
The buttercups, the little children's dower,
– Far brighter than this gaudy melon-flower!

As the verse relates, during April and May the countryside and gardens come to life. Yet it is easy to be taken unawares, as on 25 April 1908 when southern Britain was hit by a blizzard, 60cm (2ft) of snow fell in Southampton and two ships, *HMS Gladiator* and the American liner *St Paul*, collided in the English Channel, leading to the loss of 27 lives. By contrast Samuel Pepys recorded in his diary for 9 May 1669: 'This day I left off both my waistcoats by day and my waistcoat by night, it being very hot weather . . .'

The naming of months relates closely to the effects of the weather. April comes from the Latin *aperire*, meaning 'to open', while May is named after Maia, the Roman goddess of growth.

SPRING SAYINGS

Every spring month has its own sayings, including:

A windy March and a rainy April make a beautiful May.

Cloudy April dewy May.

After a wet April a dry June.

Whatever March does not want April brings along.

Bewixt April and May if there be rain, 'Tis worth more than oxen and wain [a wagon].

A THUNDERSTORM IN APRIL IS THE END OF HOAR FROST

An expression of the way in which the weather changes in April, which even if not frosty can still be cold, since it is also said, 'It is not April without a frosty crown.'

Hoar frost is essentially the frozen equivalent of dew, made up of ice crystals that condense out of air saturated with moisture and form on the ground and other surfaces whose temperature is well below freezing. The effect is a dramatic 'winter wonderland', with frost that can be so thick it looks like snow.

Meteorologists classify hoar frost into four different types. Air hoar forms on things such as tree branches and plant stems, while surface hoar is composed of fern-like ice crystals on already frozen surfaces. Beneath dry snow, depth hoar forms as cup-shaped crystals. In glacial regions, crevasse hoar forms where water vapour accumulates in deep ravines.

The end of frost was celebrated by the 17th-century poet Thomas Carew in his verse 'The Spring':

Now that the winter's gone, the earth hath lost
Her snow-white robes; and now no more the frost
Candies the grasse, or casts an ycie creame
Upon the silver Lake or Chrystall streame . . .

NE'ER CAST A CLOUT TILL MAY BE OUT

A warning not to discard your warm winter clothes too soon in spring. There is some controversy as to whether the saying refers to the month of May or to the flower of the hawthorn tree, which blooms at about this time.

Although it was probably coined much earlier, the saying was first cited by Dr Thomas Fuller, an English physician and scholar, in his *Gnomologia* of 1732, as 'Leave not off a Clout/Till May be out'. 'Clout' (also spelt 'clowt', 'cloot' or 'clute') is an old word for a piece of clothing.

Evidence that the saying refers to the month and not the blossom comes from similar, less ambiguous proverbs known in other parts of Europe, which may have migrated across the Channel. The Spanish say '*Hasta el cuarenta de mayo no te quites el sayo*' – 'Do not leave off your coat until 40 May' (in other words, 10 June) – while the French saying, '*En avril, ne te découvre pas d'un fil; en mai, fais ce qui te plait*,' means 'In April do not shed a single thread; in May do as you please.'

May, as well as being the name of the month, is the common name for the hawthorn (*Crategus monogyna*), a flower with many associations in myth and folklore. Its white, heavily scented

> To the Greeks the hawthorn flower was a symbol of luck for newlyweds. May blossoms were often held over a couple as they made their vows, the bride wore them in her headdress, the altar was strewn with them and torches made from hawthorn wood were lit to guide the pair to their nuptial chamber.

flowers were gathered for use outdoors in May Day festivities but were supposed to bring bad luck if cut and taken inside. This ill fortune was said to arise from their pungent odour, which people thought presaged death – it was said to be like that of the plague. Children were particularly discouraged from bringing the blossom indoors, being told that it would kill their mothers. Before 1752, when 1 May fell 11 days later than it does now, the flowers were nearly always open in time for the celebrations.

Flaming June sees England at play

A reference to both the weather and the summer social season, although June is an incredibly variable month that can bring snow as well as glorious warmth.

Statistically, June is England's sunniest month, and the sun is also very strong. But although the average temperature for central England is a little over 18°C (64°F), such are the contrasts of June weather that on 26 June 1976 temperatures in London reached 35°C (95°F), causing tennis balls to burst at Wimbledon, whereas on 2 June 1975, snow had fallen in many parts of the country: in Buxton, during a cricket match between Derbyshire and Lancashire, 25mm (1in) of snow settled on the outfield, stopping play for the day. In June 1983 giant hailstones fell from thunderclouds, while to the north of London 30 hours of continuous rain fell between 28 and 29 June 1999.

In the British social calendar, June was the second month of the London 'season', during which young women would 'come out' and be presented as debutantes to the monarch. A diary for 1897 details events including the Fourth of June at Eton, Royal Ascot, a fête and gymkhana at the Ranelagh Club, the start of Wimbledon and, in Portsmouth, the Jubilee Naval Review. Commenting on the weather, the diarist writes of 4 June that 'contrary to tradition, weather on the day stays fine' and 'the fine weather holds for Ascot week: too fine, from the racing point of view, since the ground is iron-hard and covered with bare patches.' As today, dress for women at Royal Ascot was all-important; in that year the main fashion point was the feather boa.

Flaming June is the title of the 1895 painting of a sleeping woman by the artist Frederick Lord Leighton, considered to be his magnum opus.

A GOOD LEAK IN JUNE SETS ALL IN TUNE

Meaning that rain in June is good for crops on farms and in gardens, helping to promote good growth; however it is less favourable for outdoor sporting events such as Wimbledon and Test cricket.

June is a wonderful month when the weather is fine but it can also be unbelievably cold and damp, although it is also said that 'June damp and warm does the farmer no harm'. A change from dry to wet weather in June is caused by the arrival of rain-bearing westerly winds, replacing the northerlies that tend to make May notoriously cold. At their extreme these westerlies can produce downpours so heavy that they are nicknamed the 'June monsoon'. Meteorologically, the best antidote to them is high pressure from the Azores, which will reliably replace rain with glorious sunny days.

Almost anything will grow in June, as this rhyme from Somerset acknowledges:

For whom the month of June is named is a matter of conjecture. Some say it honours Junius Brutus, founder of the Roman Republic. More widely accepted is the view that it is named for the Roman goddess Juno, the queen of the heavens and protector of the new moon. As befits the season, she was also goddess of fertility and childbirth. It was customary, after the birth of a baby, for a place to be laid for her at the family table.

> *Wheat or barley'll shoot in June*
> *If they bain't no higher than a spoon.*

As well as bringing on desirable crops and flowers, June rain also promotes the rapid growth of weeds. This means work for the gardener and for the farmer, who is well advised to follow the directions of the English poet and farmer Thomas Tusser, who wrote in his *Five Hundred Points of Good Husbandry*, published in 1557:

> *In June get thy wedehoke, thy knife and thy glove,*
> *And wede out such wede as the corn doth not love;*
> *Slack no time thy weding, for darth nor for cheape;*
> *Thy corn shall reward it, or ever thou reape.*

WHEN SUMMER BIRDS TAKE THEIR FLIGHT THE SEASON GOES WITH THEM

It is a sure sign that autumn has arrived when migratory birds such as the swallow, swift and house martin take their leave of the British Isles and fly to warmer climes for the winter.

The departure of the swallow was formerly observed to be more or less complete by Michaelmas, 29 September, but with warmer summers many migrants are now staying well into October, and a rare few do not leave at all. The loss of these birds from the countryside is recorded in an entry for 8 September in *Old Days in Country Places* (c. 1923): 'The swifts are the first to leave us. After August 25th I saw only a solitary one. With them went the joyousness of summer. The house-martins and swallows are, indeed, still here, but they have not the wild, glad flight of the swifts nor their joyous and pervading notes.'

Migrating birds behave in characteristic ways in autumn, lining up on telegraph wires, as R. Bosworth Smith describes in his *Bird Life and Bird Lore* of 1905: 'As autumn advances, the flocks grow in size, covering the wires for many hundred feet together, as if to discuss in concert measures for their approaching departure. Again and again you may see them launch forth from their post of vantage in a vast body, and go straight away, till they are out of sight, as though they are "off at last". But they will reappear again and again, or perhaps they may be succeeded by other flights coming southward, and resting themselves on the same wires for a time, till, one damp October morning you find that they are all really gone, in their life-long pursuit of summer sun . . .'

The fact that birds migrate in autumn and return in spring has long fascinated people. Homer's *Iliad*, composed more than 2,500 years ago, describes (in Murray's translation) 'the clamour of cranes [which] ariseth before the face of heaven, when they flee from wintry storms and measureless rain, and with clamour fly toward the streams of Ocean . . .'

In Western Europe it was believed for centuries that during the winter swallows curled up together and sank down into the mud in the bottom of pools and marshes.

September dries up ditches or breaks down bridges

A saying that describes the extremes of weather in September when summer either continues – or even revives – or is lost to day after day of heavy rain.

In Britain, strong anticyclones often become established in September, leading to settled, balmy days with clear blue skies, in contrast with August's ups and downs of wet and dry. If strong enough, the high pressure associated with these anticyclones will keep at bay gales coming from the west, which are often the remnants of hurricanes that began life in the western Atlantic.

Some Septembers, however, are marred by wet and wind, as depressions

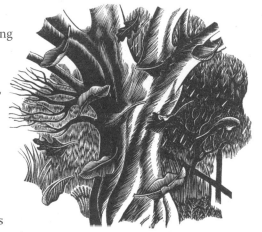

roll in, one after the other, from the Atlantic. As insurance against such weather farmers traditionally aim to have their harvest completed soon after the beginning of the month, then turn their attention to ploughing and to sowing seed for next year's crops. Thomas Tusser sums up the tasks for the month:

Thresh seed, and to farming, September doth cry,
Get plough to the field, and be sowing of rye;
To harrow the ridges, ere ever ye strike,
Is one piece of husbandry Suffolk doth like.

Fine weather that carries on beyond September is known as an Indian summer, an expression that originated in North America. A late spell of fine weather is also known as 'St Luke's summer' or 'St Martin's summer' (the feast days of these saints fall on 18 October and 11 November respectively) or an 'All Hallows summer', lasting to All Saints Day on 1 November.

A GOOD OCTOBER AND A GOOD BLAST, DO BLOW THE HOG ACORN AND MAST

As well as being food for pigs, acorns would, in prehistoric times, have been part of the human diet. Beech nuts, or mast, are not only edible but have long been enjoyed for their fine flavour, especially when roasted and salted.

When every family kept one or more pigs, such praise was apt for October winds, which when strong enough to blow acorns and beech mast from the trees helped to provide plentiful food for fattening the animals in the woods. The Greeks and Romans, as well as the Ancient Britons, commonly ate acorns, probably from necessity rather than for their flavour or nutrition. As Francis Bacon remarked in his essay *Colours of Good and Evil*, 'Acorns were good until bread was found.'

The most palatable acorns are not those of the English oak (*Quercus robur*), but of the holm or holly oak (*Q. ilex* var. *rotundifolia*), which is most common in Spain and Portugal. There, cultivated varieties are grown for their sweet acorns, which are roasted like chestnuts. In North America, acorns were eaten by both white settlers and Native Americans. For the Hupa Indians of California they were so important that a 'first fruit' ceremony was held during which acorns were ground into a

A year in which there is a prolific crop of beech nuts – and also acorns and other nuts – is called a mast year. Such years are particularly beneficial to the wild mammals and birds that depend on nature's harvest.

mush that was cooked on a ceremonial fire. Prayers were said to Yinukatsisdai, the god of vegetation, asking that the crop would not be eaten by rodents.

That the beech gets its generic Latin name *Fagus* from a Greek word meaning 'to eat' reveals its one-time importance in the diet. The fruits are like miniature sweet chestnuts, with small triangular nuts in pairs inside a prickly cup. As well as being eaten by pigs, beech nuts would once have been food for chickens and other domesticated poultry. In his 1948 work *Nuts*, F.N. Howes underlined the importance of this autumn crop: '. . . it is no exaggeration,' he says, 'to state that in times gone by the value of many an old estate in Britain was estimated more by the amount of mast the woods on it produced, which of course included acorns as well as beech nuts, than on the actual area.'

EXPECT ST MARTIN'S SUMMER, HALCYON DAYS

A reference in Shakespeare's *Henry IV* to the period of calm weather that usually descends on Europe around St Martin's Day, or Martinmas, 11 November. The name 'halcyon' is linked, through mythology, with the life of the kingfisher.

In Greek legend, Alcyone was the daughter of Aeolus, god of the winds, and the wife of Ceyx. On a journey to consult the oracle at Delphi, Ceyx was drowned, and Alcyone was so stricken with grief that she jumped into the sea to be with her beloved. The gods took pity on the pair and changed them into kingfishers, and Aeolus withheld the winds for seven days before and seven days after 21 December, the winter solstice. This period of calm is the time when Mediterranean kingfishers breed, and sailors say, 'So long as kingfishers are sitting on their eggs, no storm or tempest will disturb the ocean.'

> It is said that if the leaves of the trees and grapevines do not fall before St Martin's Day, a cold winter may be expected. Conversely, if Martinmas is fair, dry and cold, the cold in winter will not last long.

St Martin, born in the fourth century to pagan parents, travelled Europe spreading the Gospel. Legend relates that at the gate of Amiens he met a beggar with no clothes and, out of pity, took off his cloak, tore it in two, and gave one half to the man. That night, says Sulpicius Severus in his *Life of St Martin*, '... when he had gone to sleep, he saw Christ wearing the half-cloak with which he had clad the poor man.'

Sunny weather makes for autumn colour

Because sunshine in late summer boosts the sugar content of leaves, fostering the production of pigment and producing a blaze of colour. Nowhere is this more spectacular than in the woods and forests of New England.

Dry, sunny weather, ideally accompanied by cold nights, is the perfect 'recipe' for a spectacular autumn. This is helped even more by plenty of rain during the summer, keeping the leaves of deciduous trees healthy and well supplied with water and nutrients from the soil.

During the spring and summer months, leaves are green because they make the substance chlorophyll, which masks the presence of other pigments, including yellow and orange carotenoids. When chlorophyll production stops the carotenoids become visible. In addition, boosted by sunshine, the leaves – particularly those of trees such as acers and maples – make red anthocyanins. Scientists think that these act as natural sunscreens, protecting the leaves as the trees make their final attempts to make and store nutrients to tide them over the winter months.

When the work of the leaves is done, the veins that carry fluids into and out of them are gradually closed off as a layer of cells forms at the base of each leaf. These clogged veins trap sugars in the leaf and promote the production of anthocyanins. When the seal is complete, the leaf finally dies and falls to the ground, helped by the wind. Frost will kill off leaves, though some, such as those of beech and oak, linger well into winter

The fall of leaves and the coming of autumn is a time of mixed emotions, but Emily Brontë welcomed it in her poem 'Fall, Leaves', which begins:

Fall, leaves, fall; die, flowers, away;
Lengthen night and shorten day:
Every leaf speaks bliss to me,
Fluttering from the autumn tree.

In New England, famed for its fall displays, gold and yellow colours come mostly from birch, elm, poplar, redbud and hickory. These form the backdrop for the reds, magentas, maroons and even purples of red oak, hickory, ash, sugar maple, sweet gum, black gum, sourwood, sumach and dogwood.

IF THE ICE IN NOVEMBER WILL BEAR A DUCK, THERE'LL BE NOTHING AFTER BUT SLUDGE AND MUCK

November is a fickle month, which can begin with anything from an Indian summer to snowfall and end with rain or fine, frosty weather. So it is not surprising that it is the subject of many sayings and rhymes.

The vagaries of November weather make ducks somewhat unreliable forecasters, although there have been years in which this saying has proved true. In 1919, for instance, the temperature in Braemar in Scotland fell to a (then) record of -23.3°C (-10°F), but the winter that followed was very mild. Diarists and letter writers of 1710 also confirmed the saying. Horace Walpole writes on 13 November '. . . it has been fair two or three days, and this day grown cold and frosty', while Jonathan Swift, on 9 December, records such mild weather that 'The ladies were all in mobs; how do you call it? undrest; and it was the rainiest day that ever dripped.'

Frosty weather in November arrives when high pressure systems develop, resulting in sunny days but cold nights, because the absence of clouds allows heat from the earth to escape quickly as soon as the sun has set. November can also be a windy month, which can cause devastation at sea. The rhyme 'November take flail/Let ships no more sail' should perhaps have been heeded by the Royal Navy in 1703, when the fleet was caught in a great storm in the English Channel, leading to the loss of more than 8,000 sailors' lives as naval vessels and merchant ships capsized and sank (see page 171).

Autumn was condemned by the Greek physician Hippocrates as 'the mother and nurse of deadly diseases' because of the 'variable constitution of the weather'. At this time of year, he believed (as reported by Richard Saunders in 1794), 'the pores of the body are opened by a false spring heat, then suddenly closed again by autumn cold, so that many dangerous distempers are now ingender'd; such as sharp fevers, vertigoes, apoplexies, lethargies, palsies, innatious madness, windy distempers, obstructions and the like.'

November gets its name from being the ninth month of the Roman calendar. The Anglo-Saxons called it *Blotmonath*, or 'blood month', because it was when animals were slaughtered and preserved for the winter. November at its worst is epitomized in these lines by Thomas Hood:

No warmth, no cheerfulness, no healthful ease,
No comfortable feel in any member,
No shade, no shine, no butterflies, no bees,
No fruits, no flowers, no leaves, no birds –
No-vember!

Season of mists and mellow fruitfulness

The poetic expression of autumn, in John Keats' well-known verse. Autumn mists often accompany sunny days, but cold nights presage winter to come.

'To Autumn' was composed by Keats on 19 September 1819, and begins:

Season of mists and mellow fruitfulness,
Close bosom-friend of the maturing sun;
Conspiring with him how to load and bless
With fruit the vines that round the thatch-eves run;
To bend with apples the moss'd cottage-trees,
And fill all fruit with ripeness to the core;
To swell the gourd, and plump the hazel shells
With a sweet kernel; to set budding more,
And still more, later flowers for the bees,
Until they think warm days will never cease,
For Summer has o'er-brimm'd their clammy cells.

The warmth of autumn is essential for the sugars in tree fruits to mature and intensify in flavour. The shells of cobs and other nuts thicken and harden as the flesh within swells and sweetens.

A settled spell of warm weather in autumn results from the presence of an anticyclone – a mass of air that falls towards the earth and is then squeezed by high pressure. Such conditions drive out moisture from the air, making clouds disperse and leading to clear skies. Lack of cloud cover in the hours of darkness causes temperatures to drop, and as cold air falls it can lead to the formation of mists, or even dense fogs, as moisture condenses around particles in the air.

Winter's thunder makes summer's wonder

A somewhat controversial statement, and one with several contradictory versions. However, thunder in winter, especially when accompanied by snow, is both rare and remarkable.

The idea that winter thunder is a good omen for the season to come arises from the notion that the accompanying rain is helpful to crops. But the beneficial effect is not necessarily universal, for as this longer saying expresses, it was traditionally considered to be good for fruit but not for corn:

> *Winter thunder,*
> *Poor man's death, rich man's hunger.*
> *Winter thunder,*
> *Rich man's good and poor man's hunger.*

The phenomenon of 'thundersnow' – a snowstorm accompanied by thunder and lightning – is rare because thunder and lighting usually occur in summer, when warm moist air rises up into cold, turbulent air above it. But in winter, when freezing Arctic air rushes south, picking up relatively warm air from the ocean, it can bubble up and create the same effect of clashing air at different temperatures. Seeing lightning flash through the snowflakes is quite extraordinary, though the snowfall may muffle the sound of the thunder.

Whether rain or snow, 500 million litres (110 million gallons) of water can fall from the air in a single thunderstorm.

Other phenomena can accompany winter storms, as Richard Jefferies recounts in *Wild Life in a Southern County* of 1879: 'Once while walking in winter I was overtaken by a storm of rain . . . But suddenly there came an increase of darkness, and, glancing round, I saw a black cloud advancing in the teeth of the wind, and close to the earth. The trees it passed were instantly blotted out, and as it approached I could see that in the centre it bulged and hung down – or rather slanting slightly forward – in the shape of an inverted cone with the apex cut off. The bulging part was of a slaty black and the end travelled over the earth not higher than the elevation of an ordinary elm. It came up with great speed, and in a moment I was completely drenched and the field was flooded . . . Though not a perfect waterspout it was something very near it.'

A GREEN WINTER MAKES A FULL CHURCHYARD

Meaning that mild winter weather – because it does not kill or slow the multiplication of germs – results in more diseases and more deaths. In some versions of this saying, 'Christmas' and 'Yule' are specific substitutes for 'winter'.

Today, pneumonia ('the old man's friend') and influenza are winter's most lethal infections. In the past, the months from September to December were when intestinal diseases such as dysentery and typhoid were most common, and in some British villages in the 17th century they killed one in ten of the population. Disease-causing microbes multiply more slowly in cold weather, and hardly reproduce at all when the temperature is well below freezing. So stultifying is the effect of cold that Russians are reported to have discovered frozen mammoth carcasses more than 20,000 years old on which the flesh was still edible.

Even if you managed to survive the winter, the fight against disease went on, especially in the days before antibiotics, inoculations and other 'miracle' cures and preventatives. According to one saying:

> *Britain's oldest cemetery is thought to be Aveline's Hole, a cave in the Mendips where the remains of 21 humans were excavated, estimated to be more than 10,000 years old. From Saxon times churchyard burials became the norm. It was customary for good Christians to be laid to the south and east of the church; criminals, suicides and strangers would be laid to the north. This was to allow the sun to shine on the graves of the good.*

March will search,
April will try,
May will see if you live or die.

The partner of this saying is 'For a warm May the parsons pray', meaning that unseasonably warm weather would make bacteria and viruses multiply quickly, causing more deaths and plenty of funeral work for the clergy.

CHAPTER 4

NATURE'S SIGNS

Before the days of weather forecasting – and even today when we have science to rely on – it is easy to see how the behaviour of animals and plants might be used to predict the weather. As the Victorian meteorologist Richard Inwards wrote: 'The observations of naturalists, shepherds, herdsmen and others who have been brought much into contact with animals, have proved most clearly that these creatures are cognisant of approaching changes in the state of the air long before we know of their coming by other signs.'

There are literally hundreds of sayings that relate to nature's signs, and although many can be interpreted as behaviour that follows a change in the weather rather than preceding one, many others do contain at least an element of the truth, since changes in humidity, air pressure and temperature can trigger alterations in the behaviour of some species. Equally, the chances of survival, both from day to day and, over many generations, in terms of evolution, are bound to be enhanced if the consequences of severe weather can be avoided by modifications of behaviour.

However, evidence of the ability of animals to predict rain is patchy at best. So it is wise not to bank on rain if you see a pigeon bathing, a cat washing over its ears, a robin coming near the house, geese wandering, a chicken rolling in the dust or a horse stretching out its neck and sniffing the air, though many plants do close their petals when the air becomes damp. The examples selected for this chapter cover the complete range of nature's signs, from the reliable to the bizarrely inaccurate.

THE SEAGULL COMES INLAND BEFORE A STORM

A long-held view of gull behaviour and one with more than an element of truth, although these birds also come inland to scavenge in all weathers. The cries of gulls or sea mews are interpreted as signs of storms.

According to an old Scottish rhyme we should beware of any gulls not out at sea:

> *Sea-gull, sea-gull sit on the sand;*
> *It's never good weather when you're on the land.*

It is only relatively recently that seagulls have adopted the habit of flying inland to take advantage of abundant food supplies – everywhere from newly ploughed fields to rubbish dumps. The first sightings of seagulls in London were during a series of extremely cold and harsh winters in the 1880s and 1890s. Writing in *Birds in London* in 1898, W.H. Hudson remarks on the popularity of feeding these new arrivals. 'Working men and boys,' he says, 'would take advantage of the free hour at dinner time to visit the bridges and embankments, and give the scraps left from their meal to the birds. The sight of this midday crowd hurrying down to the waterside with welcome in their faces and food in their hands must,' he adds, 'have come "as an absolute revelation" to the gulls.'

To fishermen, it is the sound of the gulls that is most telling. 'The fishermen about Finisterre,' records the Victorian clergyman and amateur meteorologist C. Swainson, 'say that if you hear the gulls cry "Caré, caré, caré" it is time to wind up (*carreter*) the lines, for there will be no catch.' When out at sea, the gull's cry is generally regarded as an ill omen, and no superstitious sailor would welcome a seagull on board ship, believing it to be the incarnation of a dead soul and a harbinger of disaster.

THE WOOD ANEMONE NEVER OPENS ITS PETALS BUT WHEN THE WIND BLOWS

Hence its common name, 'windflower'. One of the earliest of spring flowers, it forms beautiful carpets on woodland floors.

The windflower, *Anemone nemorosa*, gets its scientific name from the Greek *anemos*, meaning 'wind', and *mone*, 'habitat'. Although it may not prefer windy conditions, it is certainly tolerant of stiff March breezes. It is said by some that it turns its back to the wind, just as sheep and some other animals do instinctively.

Other names for the windflower are Grandmother's nightcap and Moggie nightgown, both reflecting the shape and colour of the flowers, which are white inside and a pale purple on the outside. Within is a bunch of pale yellow stamens. The plants slowly spread by means of underground stems, confirming sites where they grow in abundance as among the oldest deciduous woodlands.

When the glow-worm lights her lamp, the air is always damp

If not always, then usually, since healthy glow-worms prefer damp locations. It will most likely be warm, too. The flashing greenish light of a colony of glow-worms is a magical sight.

Despite its common name, the glow-worm (also known as the glass-worm or shine-worm) is not a worm but a beetle, *Lampyris noctiluca*. The brightest glow-worm light comes, as the saying correctly identifies, from the insignificant-looking pale brown females, which have such stunted wing cases that they are virtually unable to fly.

The cool light comes in a steady glow from the chemical luciferin, which, when combined with water and oxygen, creates a cool, pale blue-green light.

Glow-worm larvae are also light producers; like the adults they need damp conditions to 'perform'. Their light comes in flashes, which they can keep

up for hours at a time, and although weaker than that from the adult females it is still visible up to 5m (16½ft) away. The reasons why the larvae emit light are unclear, but it seems most likely to be a means of deterring potential predators by advertising the fact that they are foul tasting.

Insects that emit light are also called fireflies; there are many species worldwide, in many of which both males and females can create light. In 13th-century Arabia they were mixed with attar of roses to make a medicine for treating ear infections. In Britain there are even anecdotes – probably fanciful – about collecting them in jars for use as emergency bicycle lamps.

LITERARY GLOW-WORMS

The glow-worm's ethereal light has obvious appeal for poets:

The glow-worm's nocturnal display, and the coolness of its light, is mentioned by Shakespeare in *Hamlet*:

The glow-worm shows the matin to be near,
And 'gins to pale his uneffectual fire.

That the light is a cool one was also correctly surmised by John Webster in *The Duchess of Malfi*:

Glories, like glow-worms, afar off
shine bright,

But looked to near, have neither heat
nor light.

The near magical nature of the glow-worm's light was evoked by Robert Herrick in his poem 'The Night-Piece, to Julia':

Her eyes the glow-worm lend thee,
The shooting-stars attend thee;
And the elves also
Whose little eyes glow,
Like sparks of fire, befriend thee.

When rooks build low, it's a sign of a wet summer to come

Rooks are sociable birds, nesting in rookeries which, at their largest, can consist of several thousand pairs. But rooks' flight patterns may be better weather forecasters than their building habits.

Country people believe it is lucky to have a rookery situated near their house. If rooks suddenly leave, it is a sign that a death has occurred.

Because rooks return to the same place year after year, and because rookeries consist of many renovated old nests as well as some new ones, it is virtually impossible to link nest height with the coming weather. More significant to the birds' wellbeing is the rookery's strict pecking order, with the oldest male bird at the centre, sheltered from the wind.

In early spring, a male rook, having found a nesting spot, sings to his partner and brings her food, then bows and calls to her before together they begin to make a new nest or renovate an untidy one. The females fight fiercely over building materials, fending off thieves. When the chicks hatch they are fed by both parents, while sentries posted at the edge of the colony (or parliament) warn when danger threatens.

Observing the autumn behaviour of rooks at Selborne in the 19th century, the naturalist Gilbert White reports their 'evening proceeding and manoeuvres' to be 'curious and amusing. Just before dusk,' he says, 'they return in long strings from the foraging of the day, and rendezvous by thousands over Selborne-down, where they wheel round in the air, and sport and dive in a playful manner, all the while exerting their voices, and making a loud cawing . . .'

When rooks 'tumble' through the air in flight, it is said that rain is on the way, while rooks that twist and turn after leaving the nest are believed to presage storms. Weather observers give these forecasts a reliability rating of 70 per cent. A noisy rookery is also said to be a sign of unsettled weather. In the Isle of Man it is believed that if rooks fly up into the mountains in dry weather, rain is near.

THE LATER THE BLACKTHORN THE BETTER THE RYE AND THE HARVEST

Meaning that a late spring is better for the crops. Both farmers and gardeners have long been aware of the dangers of the cold spring snap known as the 'blackthorn winter'.

The blackthorn, which bears the dry, sour, dark purple fruits known as sloes, is noted for the fact that its white flowers bloom well before the leaves appear, creating clouds of white in the hedgerows. On close inspection, the flowers can be seen to be very similar to those of the plum, to which it is closely related.

However, the date on which the blossoms open is very variable: it can be as early as February, but in a cold year it may not be until the end of March or even the beginning of April.

Other common names for the blackthorn (*Prunus spinosa*) include 'hedge speaks', 'quick', and 'winter picks'; 'snag bush' best describes the fact that the stems are armed with long, sharp thorns which will easily break off. In some country districts these thorns were once thought to be poisonous, probably because they could penetrate the skin, become embedded and then fester in the wounds.

Imagining Mary Queen of Scots bemoaning her imprisonment as the spring approached, Robert Burns evoked the flowering of the sloe (or 'slae') in these lines:

> *Now blooms the lily by the bank,*
> *The primrose doen the brae;*
> *The hawthorn's budding in the glen,*
> *And milk-white is the slae;*
> *The meanest hind in fair Scotland*
> *May rove their sweets amang;*
> *But I, the Queen of a' Scotland,*
> *Maun lie in prison strang!*

The fruits of the blackthorn are used in autumn to make sloe gin, which will be ready to enjoy by Christmas. The sloes are pricked with a skewer, mixed with a few spoonfuls of sugar, covered half and half by volume with gin and left to mature.

'Blackthorn winter' is the name given to the cold snap that frequently follows particularly warm early spring days that hasten the blackthorn into bloom. So common is it that William Cobbett, the farmer, journalist and campaigner, commented: 'It is a remarkable fact that there is always, that is every year of our lives, a spell of cold and angry weather just at the time this hardy little tree is in bloom. The country people call it the *Black Thorn winter* and thus it has been called, I dare say, by all the inhabitants of this island, from generation to generation, for a thousand years.'

THE HEDGEHOG CAN FORETELL A STORM

Or so it is said, because it will go into hiding when bad weather is on the way. The way in which hedgehogs build their nests is also believed to predict the direction of the wind.

Even if they are less than accurate at forecasting storms, hedgehogs certainly know how to predict the coming of winter and will make themselves hibernaculums, or winter nests, of leaves and moss. Before winter sets in these largely nocturnal creatures will forage avidly for food, and on warm late autumn days they can even be seen in daytime stocking up their food reserves.

When it comes to nest building, this is done, according to *Poor Robin's Alamanac* of 1733, with knowing regard to the direction of the prevailing winds in the coming winter:

> *Observe which way the hedgehog builds her nest,*
> *To front the north or south, or east or west;*
> *For if 'tis true that common people say,*
> *The wind will blow the quite contrary way.*
> *If by some secret art the hedgehog knows,*
> *So long before, which way the winds will blow,*
> *She has an art which many a person lacks*
> *That thinks himself fit to make our almanacks.*

How such a belief came about, and whether or not it is true, remains a mystery. But other sages have taken note of the hedgehog's behaviour during and after nest building, as propounded in the 17ᵗʰ-century *Husbandman's Practice*: 'The hedgehog commonly hath two holes or vents in his den or cave, the one towards the south and the other towards the north; and look which of them he stops – thence will great storms and winds follow.'

BEETLES COME OUT BEFORE THE RAIN

They may do, depending on what type of beetle they are, but most reliable of all are the rain beetles of North America. Other more common beetles, such as the chafers, are particularly active on summer evenings when, even if it does not rain, the air is heavy with humidity.

If you turn over a beetle that has fallen and landed on its back you will have good luck and, say some, will be protected from toothache.

The reddish brown rain beetle, native to the western United States from Oregon to California, spends most of its life underground, emerging from its burrow only in response to a fall of rain or snow. The females have only vestigial wings, while the winged males may fly just once a year – while it is raining – in order to find a mate.

In Britain, the unusual behaviour of beetles with regard to the weather is most often associated with black ground beetles, traditionally known as clock beetles. When flying in circles and buzzing, these are said to indicate fine weather rather than rain. Zoologically, these members of the family Carabidae belong to a massive variety of species, but all will typically run for cover whenever the stones or logs under which they normally hide during daylight hours are disturbed.

Spiders fall from their cobwebs before it rains

Or if not, may certainly take shelter when rain is falling, although it is said that if they continue working in the rain the weather is sure to clear. Spiders' webs are seen at their most dramatic when covered in dew on a fine autumn morning.

As weather forecasters, spiders are more likely to indicate what is in store by the type of web they weave. When rain or wind are imminent, they tend to make their fixing or 'frae' lines short, while in fine weather these are long – sometimes more than 1m (3ft). At the approach of a tempest spiders are said to undo their webs, though a more rational explanation is that the strong wind on which the storm approaches is the destructive force.

A summer that is neither too hot nor too cold, nor too wet nor too dry, will produce a plethora of webs in September, as witnessed by the naturalist Gilbert White. 'On September 21st, 1741,' he records, 'being then on a visit, and intent on field diversion, I rose before daybreak: when I came into the enclosures, I found the stubbles and clover-grounds matted all over with thick coat of cobweb, in the meshes of which a copious and heavy dew hung so plentifully that the whole face of the country seemed, as it were, covered with two or three setting-nets drawn one over another.'

If the night ahead is going to be calm the spider will, it is said, adjust its web between 6.00 and 7.00 pm precisely!

House spiders thrive outdoors in summer but will come indoors for warmth and shelter in autumn when the nights get chilly. The presence of long strands of spiders' webs on the grass is said in Ireland to indicate that there will be a frost at night, while from America comes the same idea in the saying: 'Spiders' webs floating at autumn sunset bring a night frost – this you may bet.'

The link between spiders and rain is captured in this old children's rhyme, traditionally accompanied by appropriate hand movements, including tickling:

> *Incy Wincy Spider climbed up the spout,*
> *Down came the rain and washed the spider out.*
> *Out came the sun and dried up all the rain,*
> *Incy Wincy Spider climbed up the spout again.*

WHEN SHEEP TURN THEIR BACKS TO THE WIND IT IS A SIGN OF RAIN

Or of the wind blowing uncomfortably in their faces. Since the weather is linked so closely to the health and safety of their flocks grazing out on the hills, it is not surprising that shepherds are the source of much traditional weather lore.

Sheep were first domesticated in southwest Asia around 8000 BC and now exist in more than 40 different breeds. Mouflons – wild sheep – can still be found in remote parts of Europe such as the mountains of Corsica but have never been native to Britain, where sheep were introduced in domesticated form some time before the Roman invasion. Hardiest of all are the hill breeds such as the Cheviot and Blackface, but the insulating properties of their fleece make all sheep tolerant of cold weather.

Aratus, the Greek poet of the third century BC, had plenty to say about the behaviour of sheep in his *Phaenomena*, translated by John Lamb in 1848:

> *The shepherd, as afield his charge he drives,*
> *From his own flock prognostics oft derives.*
> *When they impetuous seek the grassy plain,*
> *He marks the advent of some storm or rain;*
> *And when grave rams and lambkins full of play*
> *Butt at each other's heads in mimic fray;*
> *When the horned leaders stamp the dusty ground*
> *With their forefeet – all fours the young ones bound;*
> *When homeward, as the shades of night descend,*
> *Reluctantly and slow their way they wend,*
> *Stray from the flock, and linger one by one,*
> *Heedless of shepherd's voice and missive stone.*

One of the oldest weather guides in print, first published in 1670 as *The Shepherd's Legacy*, is *The Country Calendar, or The Shepherd of Banbury's Rules to judge of the Changes of the Weather*. The shepherd in question styled himself as John Claridge, though the work has also been attributed to a Dr John Campbell, whose name appeared on the title page of an enlarged edition in 1744. In subsequent versions of the guide, meteorologists have put their own interpretations on the shepherd's sayings

Sheep bleat little except at lambing time to communicate with their young, but it is an old saying that if they bleat greatly at night then severe weather is to be expected. If they gambol and fight this is said to presage a change in the weather.

When black snails on the road you see, then on the morrow rain will be

Or, more probably, it has rained already. Because they need damp conditions to survive, all snails, whatever their colour, are more active when it is wet.

As gardeners will testify, snails are more active by night than by day. In the hours of darkness they emerge to feed on leaves and fruits, mosses, algae and all kinds of decaying matter. During the day, in dry weather and over the winter, they will remain within their shells and, if conditions are severe, create a protective plug over the aperture.

The emergence of snails from their shells, accompanied by the raising of their horns, has inspired other weather rhymes relating to the onset of rain. From Somerset comes:

> *Snail, snail, put out your horn,*
> *We want some rain to grow our corn.*
> *Out, horn, out.*

Other aspects of snail behaviour are believed to be significant to events beyond the weather. If, before going to bed, a girl picks up a black snail by the horns and throws it over her shoulder into the ashes of the fire, in the morning it will have left behind the initials of her future husband. And if a snail comes indoors, especially into a dairy, then it is a sign of death.

Petrels Gathered Under the Stern of a Ship Foretell Foul Weather

These birds get their reputation for weather forecasting from their habit of appearing suddenly beside a ship before, or more commonly during, a storm.

Except when they are breeding, most species of storm petrel live their whole lives at sea, feeding on plankton, krill and fish, and coming close to the shore only at night. To superstitious sailors, however, their presence bodes ill – often rightly so – because in stormy weather they will follow ships, scavenging for food scraps thrown overboard.

Because of their association with foul weather and misfortune, storm petrels are commonly called 'Mother Carey's chickens'. This comes, supposedly, from the words *Mater Cara*, meaning 'Dear Mother' (a name for the Blessed Virgin Mary, to whom sailors' lives were believed to be entrusted), uttered by sailors when storms strike. When hovering close to the ocean surface to feed, storm petrels patter their feet on the water and look as though they are 'walking' on the waves. For this reason they are often called St Peter's birds, a reference to the occasion when the disciple's faith led him to obey Jesus's command to walk on water. Another theory is that the name comes from their 'pitter pattering' on the water.

Wilson's petrel, *Oceanites oceanicus*, named for the Scottish-American ornithologist James Wilson, is the world's most abundant seabird. It gets its genus name from the Greek meaning 'son of the sea'. It breeds in the Antarctic but may migrate as far as the north Atlantic during the southern winter.

FORETELL THE WEATHER WITH A LEECH IN A JAR

The 'Leech Barometer' or 'Tempest Prognosticator', a bizarre 19th-century contraption for foretelling the weather, was the invention of a Dr George Merryweather. It relied on the way in which the creatures respond to the approach of rain.

Dr Merryweather of Whitby was inspired in his invention by lines from the poem 'Signs of Rain' by Edward Jenner: 'The leech disturbed is newly risen;/Quite to the summit of his prison.' Merryweather displayed his Leech Barometer at the Great Exhibition of 1851. It consisted of 12 pint jars half filled with water, with a medicinal leech in each one. The jars were arranged in a circle beneath a large bell, which could be struck by a small hammer connected to each jar with wire attached to a piece of whalebone. If the leeches were agitated by the approach of a storm they would ascend to the necks of their jars, dislodging the pieces of whalebone and causing the bell to ring.

In his *Weather Lore* of 1898 Richard Inwards provides detailed descriptions of the movements of the leeches in their jars:

1. If the leech take up a position in the bottle's neck, rain is at hand.
2. If he form a half-moon, when he is out of the water and sticking to the glass, sure sign of tempest.
3. If he is in continual movement, thunder and lightning soon.
4. If he seem as if trying to raise himself from the surface of the water, a change in the weather.
5. If he move slowly close to one spot, cold weather.
6. If he move rapidly about, expect strong wind when he stops.

7. If he lie coiled up on the bottom, fine, clear weather.

8. If forming a hook [as illustrated], clear and cold weather.

9. If in a fixed position, very cold weather is certain to follow.

Although he lobbied for the establishment of his devices around the coast of Britain in order to predict storms, Merryweather's dream remained unfulfilled; the government opted instead for the storm glass invented by Admiral Robert Fitzroy.

The original device, elaborately fashioned in the style of an Indian temple, no longer exists, but a replica was made for the Festival of Britain in 1951 and is now in Whitby Museum. A working model can also be seen at the Barometer Museum in Okehampton in Devon.

If the owl hoots at night expect fair weather

The voice of the owl has long been taken as a weather sign, though it has other dark and melancholy associations. Its hooting is one of many bird calls thought to indicate the weather that is to come.

Reflecting on the behaviour of owls, the Renaissance scientist and philosopher Francis Bacon wrote: 'The whooping of the owl was thought by the ancients to betoken a change of weather, from fair to wet, or from wet to fair. But with us an owl, when it whoops clearly and freely, generally shows fair weather, especially in winter.'

As with other birds, the calls that owls make may be territorial: that is, they are warnings to others to stay away. Alternatively, a bird may call to contact its mate or young, or to advertise its availability for breeding. Owls of different species have quite distinct 'voices'. The barn owl, for instance, produces a sound that is more a screech than a hoot. Of British owls, those with the loudest and most distinctive hoots are the brown or tawny owls, which, like other nocturnal birds, are more likely to be hunting when the weather is fair and their rodent prey active and easily accessible.

The shriek of an owl is widely believed to be an omen of death. An equally bad sign is to see an owl flying during daylight hours. To counteract evil, the remedy is to turn money over in your pocket or to turn an article of clothing inside out.

AVIAN VOICES

According to weather lore, you should also listen out for these other bird signals – or note their absence:

Whistling parrots indicate rain.

If birds are silent, expect thunder.

Guinea fowls squall more than usual before rain.

When quails are heard in the evening, expect fair weather next day.

The peafowl utters loud cries before a storm – and selects a low perch.

The crow, raven and jackdaw, calling late in the day, indicate a storm.

THE STRUTTING PEACOCK YAWLS AGAINST THE RAIN

Or, as the rhyme goes, 'When the peacock loudly bawls, soon we'll have both rain and squalls.' The peacock, renowned for spectacular displays of its fine tail feathers, is believed to bring on rain with its dancing.

The peacock is a dubious weather forecaster, and in fact makes so much noise, so much of the time, that it would be impossible to believe it reliable. The males are particularly raucous when they are trying to attract a mate – the females answer in lower, slightly more melodious tones. However, in its native India the peacock's mating season coincides with the arrival of the monsoon, which may partly explain its association with rain. The month of Shraavana in the Hindu calendar is traditionally the time for rain songs and peacock dances.

In *Love's Martyr*, an allegory of 1601 by the mysterious poet Robert Chester, the ways of the peacock are perfectly described:

> *The proud sun-braving peacocke with his feathers,*
> *Walkes all along, thinking himself a king,*
> *And with his voice prognosticates all weathers,*
> *Although God knowes but badly he doth sing;*
> *But when he looks downe to his base black feete,*
> *He droops, and is ashamed of things unmeete.*

Despite its noisiness, the peacock has always been prized for its feathers, particularly those of the male's tail with their iridescent blues and greens and startling 'eyes', although many people believe it is unlucky to bring them indoors because they are associated with the evil eye.

The peacock was a popular centrepiece of the medieval banquet, when spectacular 'illusion foods' were de rigueur: the bird would be carefully skinned before roasting to keep its plumage intact, and then 're-dressed' in its gorgeous feathers and made to stand on the table as if still alive.

Expect stormy weather when ants travel in lines and fair weather when they scatter

A very poor way of predicting the weather, since when they come out of the nest ants tend to walk in single file come rain or shine. However, the behaviour of flying ants is certainly linked to weather conditions.

Ants tend to travel along the ground in lines because they follow scent or pheromone trails left by their co-habitants as they go about foraging for food. This is just one of the ways in which ant colonies are able to grow and thrive, as wingless workers bring food back to the nest. As this verse by Isaac Watts reveals, even the busy way in which they do this is to some extent dependent on the weather:

They don't wear their time out in sleeping or play,
But gather up corn in a sunshiny day,
*   ' And for winter they lay up their stores:*
They manage their work in such regular forms,
One would think they foresaw all the frosts and the storms,
*   And so brought their food within doors.*

As Watts correctly suggests, ants do indeed store up food for the winter months. If they start enlarging and rebuilding their nests in preparation for winter as early as July, it is said that an early and cold winter will follow.

In hot weather ants will bury themselves deeper than usual to keep cool. It is also believed by some that an open ant hole indicates clear weather, a closed one an approaching storm.

Within the nest of the black garden ant, most of the resident males (the workers) are sterile and wingless. A few, however, are fertile and winged, and when these hatch they are fed and pampered by their hard-working nest mates. The workers monitor the weather and, when conditions are perfect in terms of warmth and humidity, usually in late summer, release both the flying males and the queens to swarm and mate.

Noting this behaviour, the naturalist Gilbert White wrote on 2 October 1795: 'Flying ants, male and female, usually swarm and migrate on hot sunny days in August and September; but this day a vast emigration took place in my garden and myriads came forth, in appearance from the drain which goes under the fruit wall; filling the air and the adjoining trees and shrubs with their numbers. The females were full of eggs. The late swarming is probably owing to the backward wet season.'

DANDELIONS CLOSE THEIR BLOSSOMS BEFORE A STORM

One of many plants whose behaviour is believed to predict the weather. While they may not be accurate forecasters, dandelions certainly keep their heads closed in poor weather, opening them wide when the sun shines.

The dandelion, one of the commonest plants of the countryside and a persistent weed of lawns, beds and borders, is so hardy that it can be found in flower almost all year round, whatever the weather. In times past, when winters were generally more severe, note was taken of the date on which the buds opened, for as Richard Inwards says in *Weather Lore*: 'When dandelions bloom early in spring, there will be a short season. When they bloom late, expect a dry summer.' The arrival of the flower is a sure herald of spring, as Walt Whitman expressed in his poem 'The First Dandelion' in 1888:

> *Simple and fresh and fair from winter's close emerging,*
> *As if no artifice of fashion, business, politics had ever been,*
> *Forth from its sunny nook of shelter'd grass –*
>   *innocent, golden, calm as the dawn,*
> *The spring's first dandelion shows its trustful face.*

It is certainly a fact of plant physiology that the dandelion flower is sensitive to changes in humidity, which explains why it will close its petals before and during rain. As well as the flowers, the seed heads or 'clocks' of the dandelion are also used to forecast the weather. When there is no wind, yet the down flies off the seed heads, then it is said that rain is on the way.

Oak before ash, only a splash, ash before oak, soak, soak, soak

A rhyme long used to predict the summer weather from the order in which these two trees come into leaf, but not very reliable, as the ash is almost always second of the two, whatever the weather to come.

Britain's Woodland Trust, using records going back to the 18th century, bears out the dubious nature of this prediction. Even though the ash bears its delicate sprays of tufted flowers before the leaves of either tree emerge, it is rarely in leaf before the oak. However, British summers are now becoming hotter and drier, so it may be premature to write off the forecast altogether.

The English oak (*Quercus robur*) can live for well over 500 years – and reputedly as long as 1,000 – and many have become landmarks, such as Gospel Oak in North London. The ash (*Fraxinus excelsior*), easy to recognize in winter from its black buds and silver grey bark, is sometimes called the Queen of the Forest; in Scandinavian mythology Yggdrasil, the tree of life, was an ash tree.

Oak Apple Day on 29 March is celebrated as the date in 1660 on which

At the end of summer, oak is one of the last trees to shed its leaves, which some see as a portent, as in the rhyme:
'If on the trees the leaves still hold,
The coming winter will be cold.'

the exiled King Charles II returned triumphant to London. He is connected with the oak because of the tree at Boscobel in which he hid while escaping from Parliamentary soldiers after the Battle of Worcester. An oak 'apple' is a gall or swelling on the tree created in late spring by a wasp larva. In Spain it is traditional to examine the galls when wheat is ready for harvest. If a maggot is found within then it is a sign that there will be a good yield; if the insect has already hatched the reverse is true.

Cows lie down when it's going to rain

They do – and they don't! In other words they are poor weather forecasters, though some farmers claim that their cows do predict storms by exhibiting bad-tempered behaviour. Cows with any sense will take shelter from a downpour by standing or lying down under the trees.

The truth about cow behaviour is that come rain or shine they generally stand up to eat in the morning and evening and lie down – for anything up to 12 hours – to chew the cud for the rest of the day and night. Being herd animals, what one does, all (or most) do, so when you pass a field of cows you are very likely to see them all eating or all chewing. Cattle chew the cud to get maximum benefit from hard-to-digest grass, using their four stomachs in turn.

Bullocks (as well as goats and pigs), according to Aratus, exhibit weather-predicting behaviour of which the farmer should be well aware:

> *The herdsmen too, while yet the skies are fair,*
> *Warned by their bullocks, for the storm prepare –*
> *When with rough tongue they lick their polished hoof,*
> *When bellowing loud they seek the sheltering roof,*
> *When from the yoke at close of day released,*
> *On his right side recumbs the wearied beast:*
> *When keenly pluck the goats the oaken bough;*
> *And deeply wallows in the mire the sow.*

A WATCH ON THE WEATHER

Many other forms of cow behaviour are believed to predict the weather:

If cows bellow at night, expect snow.

To predict rain, look at a heifer's tail. If it is held upright, then showers are on the way.

When a cow scratches its ear a shower is near.

Rain is predicted if cows stop and shake their feet, refuse to go to pasture in the morning or low and gaze at the sky.

If the cock crows on going to bed, he's sure to rise with a watery head

A far from accurate means of forecasting, but one that is widely believed in country districts. Other behaviour of cocks and hens is also closely observed for both short- and long-term weather predictions.

> At Christmas, the cock is believed to raise his voice all night long to welcome the Christ Child.

Cocks will crow at all times of the day – and at night too – but crowing is most often a sign that dawn is breaking. In ancient times the cockerel was believed to wait quietly for the morning, banishing the Devil by raising its voice at first light. A cock crowing late at night was thought to presage death.

As to other behaviour, fowls are rich in the signs they are alleged to give to the ardent weather watcher. As Richard Inwards recounts in *Weather Lore*: 'When they look towards the sky, or roost in daytime, expect rain; but if they dress their feathers during a storm, it is about to cease; while their standing on one

leg is considered a sign of cold weather. When fowls collect together, and pick or straighten their feathers, expect a change.'

The time at which the birds lose their feathers in spring is also held to be significant, according to the rhyme:

If the cock moult before the hen,
We shall have weather thick and thin;
But if the hen moult before the cock,
We shall have weather hard as a block.

OBSERVATIONS FROM THE CHICKEN COOP

More signs that may sometimes be accurate predictions:

If cocks crow late and early, clapping their wings unusually, rain is expected.

If fowls roll in the sand, rain is at hand.

If the cock drinks in summer, it will rain a little after.

If fowls grub in the dust and clap their wings, or if their wings droop, or if they crowd into a house, it indicates rain.

If the fowls huddle together outside the henhouse instead of going to roost, there will be wet weather.

A bee was never caught in a shower

Simply because it is clever enough to get home before rain sets in. Bees are also thought to be able to time their swarming so as to avoid storms.

The behaviour of bees is so extraordinary that it is hardly surprising that as well as being able to find the best sources of nectar and communicate – simply by patterns of movement – their whereabouts to others in the hive, bees have a 'sense' of the changes in the weather. They are almost certainly able to perceive changes in humidity, and the direction and strength of the wind, and to adjust their behaviour accordingly.

Bees are less likely to travel far when bad weather is approaching, as this anonymous verse relates:

When bees to distance wing their flight,
Days are warm and skies are bright;
But when their flight ends near their home,
Stormy weather is sure to come.

The 'wisdom' of bees has long been appreciated. As Virgil observed in Book IV of his *Georgics*, written in AD 29 (translated by Joseph Addison):

By turn they watch, by turns with curious eyes
Survey the heavens, and search the clouded skies
To find out breeding storms and tell what tempests rise.

Swarming, as beekeepers have observed, is often associated with the sudden onset of a spell of bad weather during which the bees are confined to the hive. If this has followed a period of productive foraging, it seems to be a powerful trigger for the queen and the other bees to leave the hive in search of a new venue for the colony.

When swallows fly low, rain is on the way

Although swallows rarely fly very high in the sky, these graceful birds have been used as weather predictors since ancient times.

The Roman poet Virgil was one of the earliest recorders of typical swallow behaviour:

> *Wet weather seldom hurts the most unwise;*
> *So plain the signs, such prophets are the skies . . .*
> *The swallow skims the river's watery face;*
> *The frogs renew the croaks of their loquacious race.*

On a fine day, as they hunt for flying insects, which they scoop up into their wide, deep bills, swallows will alternately glide high in the air, to catch groups of weak prey that have been drawn up from the ground by warm air currents, and down over open ground or water, where larger insects abound. But when the air

pressure falls and the air is full of moisture (whether or not it is going to rain) insects descend much nearer the ground, as do the swallows that pursue them.

When it's wet and windy, insects go to ground or stay lodged in vegetation or in the lee of a hedge or wall. Then swallows have to travel farther from their nests – to places such as ponds or sewage farms – and will sometimes pick insects off trees or even forage for food on the ground. Near the coast, especially when it's windy, you can see swallows low on the wing catching sandhoppers and flies.

> *When, in spring, there are more swifts than swallows on show then it is said that a hot, dry summer is expected.*

A CUCKOO IN SEPTEMBER, NO ONE EVER CAN REMEMBER

A tribute to the migratory habits of the cuckoo, though in some country districts people once believed that in the autumn cuckoos changed into hawks in order to survive the winter in Britain.

This saying is the last line of a rhyme with several versions, one of which is:

> *Cuckoo, cuckoo, pray what do you do?*
> *In April I open my bill*
> *In May I sing both night and noon*
> *In June I change my tune*
> *In July away I fly*
> *In August away I must.*

As the rhyme rightly relates, the call of the cuckoo (*Cuculus canorus*) is most persistent in early summer, changing subtly to a 'Cuk-cuck-oo' later in the season. The cuckoo is renowned as a brood parasite: it lays its huge eggs in the nests of small birds, including meadow pipits and hedge sparrows. Each egg hatches into a large

Cuckoo spit (also known as frog spit) is the frothy white exudate deposited on plant leaves by insects, especially those of the froghopper family Cercopidae, to protect their larvae.

chick with a massive yellow gape, irresistible to the rearing instincts of its foster parents, which spend from 17 to 21 exhausting days bringing it food.

BIRDS OF OMEN

Like magpies, cuckoos are the objects of many superstitions:

The number of consecutive calls you hear is the number of years until you will marry.

If you hear a cuckoo before the swallows have arrived, sorrow lies ahead.

When you hear the first cuckoo, look under your shoe. You will find a hair the same colour as that of your spouse to be.

Whatever you are doing when you hear the first cuckoo you will do all year.

If you have money in your pocket when you hear the first cuckoo then you will have wealth all year.

The luckiest time to hear a first cuckoo is on Easter morning.

WHEN THE SQUIRREL EATS NUTS ON THE TREE EXPECT A WARM WINTER

The theory is that if, in autumn, the squirrel is eating nuts rather than storing them, it is predicting mild weather to come. In fact, generally milder winters now make it easier for squirrels to find food all year round.

Hazel nuts, beech mast and acorns are the favourite foods of squirrels, and they habitually store surpluses in tree hollows or underground. However, they will also eat roots and shoots, and they not only raid garden vegetable patches – for everything from broad beans and peas to sweetcorn – but steal nuts from bird feeders with remarkable persistence and dexterity.

In Britain the most common squirrel is the grey, *Sciurus carolinensis*, a voracious American immigrant whose habits have earned it such derogatory descriptions as 'tree rat' and 'rat with attitude'. The native red squirrel (*S. vulgaris*, pictured), now found only in pine forests in isolated parts of Scotland and Wales, in East Anglia, on the Isle of Wight and on Brownsea Island, is smaller and daintier, with attractive colouring and long ear tufts. Although threatened in Britain, the red squirrel remains abundant elsewhere in Europe.

As grey squirrels are today, the reds were once hunted (and often eaten). They were even accused of entering homes and eating woollen garments. In many

The squirrel gets its name from a Greek word meaning 'shade tail' but in the 16th century it was, like the rabbit, known as a 'bun'. From the animal's habit of stowing away food, human hoarders and collectors are commonly called 'squirrels'.

parts of the country a squirrel hunt was part of the ritual Boxing Day celebrations. Like the hedgehog, the squirrel is supposed to be able to alter the position of the entrance to its nest (or dray) according to the direction of the wind, as described by the 16th-century French poet Guillaume de Salluste Du Bartas:

There skips the squirrill, seeming weather-wise,
Without beholding of heav'n's twinkling eyes:
For, knowing well which way the wind will change,
He shifts the portall of his little grange.

IF THE LADYBIRD HIBERNATES, THE WINTER WILL BE HARSH

Remarkably, this saying does contain an element of truth, at least for the orange ladybird. Traditionally, the spots on this much-revered insect are also believed to be able to predict the value of the harvest – and the source of true love.

For more than a decade, a zoologist at Cambridge University named Michael Majerus studied the ability of the orange ladybird (which has 16 white spots) to predict the weather of the coming winter by the way in which it hibernates. If the

ladybird spends its winter above
ground, nestling in a small crevice
in a sheltered position – such as the
branch of a smooth-surfaced tree
like the sycamore, at least 1m (3ft)
from the ground – then the winter
will be mild. But if it hibernates on

> The ladybird (known as the ladybug
> in North America) is thought to be
> sacred to the Virgin Mary; it is also known
> as 'God Almighty's cow'.

the ground among dead, dry leaves then a harsh winter is to be expected.
To date this has proved a totally accurate forecast.

As to the value of the harvest, in Norse and other northern European
mythologies it is believed that if ladybirds seen in summer have seven spots or
fewer then the harvest will be abundant and prices low. Again, there may be
some truth in this, for many of the ladybirds that have more than seven spots
are avid fungi feeders and thrive in wet summers, when crop-damaging fungal
diseases are rife and the harvest is likely to be poor.

When it comes to true love, the ladybird – which 'flies away home' – is
believed to take wing to help locate a perfect mate. According to country ritual
the insect should be gently blown off the hand or tossed into the air while
chanting the words:

> Fly away east, fly away west,
> Show me where lives the one I love best.

Alternatively, you can use this old rhyme:

> Bishop, Bishop Barnabee,
> Tell me when my wedding be;
> If it be tomorrow day,
> Take your wings and fly away.

Plenty of holly berries presage a cold winter

A widely held view, though in fact a good crop of holly berries, or berries of any kind, is more likely to reflect the weather that is past, not what is to come.

It is moist, warm weather during spring and summer, and a lack of winds to blow off blossom before it can be pollinated, that is likely to produce a plethora of berries in autumn and winter, rather than the weather to come. But whether the crop is large or small, holly is one of the many trees whose berries provide vital sustenance for birds over the winter months. If the 'cold winter' theory were true, it would be reasonable to assume that in the exceptional winters of 1947 and 1963 birds would have had a better chance of survival – which in fact they did not. The winter of 1989–90 was one of the mildest of the past century, yet the autumn of 1989 produced one of the heaviest berry crops ever recorded. Conversely, another bumper berry crop preceded the long cold winter of 2009–10.

The role of holly in the winter landscape was beautifully captured by the Victorian poet Augusta Webster:

> *'Tis a brave tree. While round its boughs in vain*
> *The warring wind of January bites and girds,*

Holly is used as a Christmas decoration due to the long-held belief that the Cross was made from holly wood and that as a 'punishment' it now has thorny leaves and blood-red berries. Another legend relates that it was used to make Christ's crown of thorns and that thereafter its berries, once yellow, turned to red.

It holds the clusters of its crimson grain,
A winter pasture for the shivering birds.
Oh, patient holly, that the children love,
No need for thee of smooth blue skies above:
Oh, green strong holly, shine amid the frost;
Thou dost not lose one leaf for sunshine lost.

Before a snowstorm, hares take to open country

A Scottish saying that probably refers more to the winter behaviour of hares in general than to the weather in particular. For no obvious reason, hares are the subject of numerous superstitions and are even regarded as witches in disguise.

Hares are solitary creatures and fast runners, and can be seen racing – haring – across the fields in winter, foraging for root crops to sustain them through the cold. Unlike rabbits, they do not burrow but rest in hollows or 'forms' in long grass, from which they will start up if disturbed. They are usually seen in groups only in spring, which is the mating season; the frantic 'boxing' of hares, from which the expression 'mad March hare' derives, is most usually played out between a male and an unreceptive female. The most common hare in Britain is the brown hare (*Lepus europaeus*), identified by its long black-tipped ears. Occasionally albino or white hares arise, which in country districts are thought to represent the souls of people who have died in tragic circumstances. The mountain hare (*L. timidus*), found in the Scottish islands, sports a white coat only in winter. The summer coat of this creature, whose ears are markedly shorter than those of the brown hare, is grey.

The hare may not always run fast when the weather is cold, as John Keats noted in his poem 'The Eve of St Agnes' (20 January):

> *– Ah, bitter chill it was!*
> *The owl, for all his feathers, was a-cold;*
> *The hare limp'd trembling through the frozen grass,*
> *And silent was the flock in woolly fold.*

The Easter 'bunny' is in fact a hare. Easter is named from the pagan festival Eastre, held at the vernal equinox in celebration of the goddess of the dawn, whose sacred animal was the hare

HARES IN LORE AND SUPERSTITION

A very large number of beliefs have gathered about hares:

Witches disguise themselves as hares so that they can milk cattle undetected.

A hare's paw carried in a right hand pocket is a lucky charm and will ward off rheumatism.

If a pregnant woman sets eyes on a hare her baby will be born with the facial deformity known as a 'hare lip'.

If a fisherman sees a hare on the way to his boat he will turn tail and go home. The same is true for a miner on his way to the pit.

A hare seen running down the street portends a fire.

CHAPTER 5

EXTREME WEATHER

E xtreme weather not only makes the news but alters the landscape and can affect whole nations. In Britain it is common to compare the weather to notable events in living memory – the 'drought summer of '76', the 'winter of '63' or the 'great storm of '87' – but every generation has experienced similar extremes. Historical records document the violent storm of 1287, which swept away the old town of Winchelsea in Kent and the island on which it stood; it also flooded East Anglia and helped to begin the formation of the Norfolk Broads. But the worst storm of all, described in this chapter, was the one of late November 1703, in which hurricane-force winds led to the loss of thousands of lives.

Long periods of extreme weather have influenced the course of history. It was the drenching summers of the mid-1800s that brought on potato blight, which caused famine in Ireland and triggered mass emigration to America. Yet a century before, during the Little Ice Age, Ireland had been colonized by Scottish Presbyterians searching for milder weather. And is it a coincidence that the weather was warm over Europe as the Roman Empire began to burgeon but turned cold, causing widespread famine, in the years before it fell?

Predicting extreme weather is far from easy, although experts can forecast to some extent the effects of events such as El Niño, the tropical phenomenon in which the Pacific becomes warmer than normal, inevitably leading to floods and droughts in Asia, Australia and southern Africa. The Atlantic hurricane season and the Asian monsoon are also relatively easy to predict, but despite the best efforts of the forecasters the weather can surprise us time after time.

Beware the Oak it Draws a Stroke, Avoid an Ash it Counts the Flash

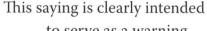

This saying is clearly intended to serve as a warning against sheltering under a tree when there is lightning about, though it ends with a recommendation: 'Creep under the thorn it can save you from harm.'

Whatever the species, it is extremely wise to stay away from the shelter of any tall tree, especially an isolated one, when lightning is about. The reason is that trees can act as conductors and possibly allow lightning to enter your body. Even more important is to avoid touching anything metal, such as a golf club, which will act as an even more efficient lightning conductor. Because lightning tends to strike the tallest objects in its vicinity, the best advice is to crouch as low as possible, ideally on something dry, and to avoid touching the ground with your hands.

Lightning is a discharge of electricity whose head or 'leader' can travel at speeds of up to 60,000m/sec (130,000mph) and reach temperatures as hot as 30,000°C (54,000°F). This is hot enough to melt sand composed of silica, which, when it cools, forms natural hollow glass tubes known as fulgurites, or petrified lightning, because of their resemblance to fossils. The colour of fulgurites, which are usually coated with particles of sand, varies from black, brown and green to translucent white. The longest one yet found, in northern Florida, measures 5m (16¼ft) long.

The mythologies of almost every culture attribute lightning to a deity as the manifestation of his wrath. In Greek culture, Zeus was the god of thunder and lightning, and any spot struck by lightning immediately became sacred. In Persian mythology the Maruts rode through the heavens in chariots of lightning, striking down everything from forests to cattle and humans.

FOR HOME AND BODY

Throughout the world, a variety of rituals are undertaken to help keep the home safe from the ravages of lightning:

Burn a Yule log on Christmas Eve and the house will be safe for the coming year. (Scandinavia)

A piece of hawthorn cut on Maundy Thursday will protect both a home and the people in it. (Shropshire, England)

A toothpick made from the wood of a tree struck by lightning will cure toothache. (Maryland, USA)

A piece of wood from a tree splintered by lightning, carried in the pocket, will possess extraordinary strength. (England)

A charred log from a midsummer bonfire kept in the home will afford protection. (Germany)

Ashes from the same bonfire can be equally efficacious. (Picardy, France)

AT A COMING STORM YOUR HOLLOW TOOTH WILL RAGE

Although teeth are more likely to be sensitive to cold weather than to a storm. Certainly, many people correctly sense the approach of rain by the onset of arthritic or rheumatic pain.

The 'hollow tooth' of the expression is most likely to be one with an unfilled cavity. If a coming storm affects the nervous system – which indeed it may – then it is quite possible that a tooth might hurt more. In older people, whose gums have receded somewhat, so exposing the nerves, breathing in very cold air can also be a trigger for pain.

It is now acknowledged that some rheumatism sufferers are weather-sensitive, and reliably report more pain on damp, cold days. Some can also 'feel' nearby thunderstorms; once the weather stabilizes, so their pain abates. Researchers have even built climate chambers, and maintain that at least 70 per cent of rheumatism sufferers are adversely affected by impending rain. Or, as poetically put by Samuel Butler in his 17th-century satire *Hudibras*:

> *For as old sinners have all points*
> *O' th' compass in their bones and joints,*
> *Can by their pangs and aches find*
> *All turns and changes of the wind,*
> *And better than by Napier's bones*
> *Feel in their own the age of moons.*

Almost certainly less reliable than rheumatic pain is 'the deceptive appearance of motes or small flies before the eyes' said to 'presage rain and storms'.

(Napier's bones were rods arranged on a form of abacus used for calculations.)

A HAILSTORM BY DAY DENOTES FROST AT NIGHT

A prediction that could possibly be correct in winter, but not during the warmer months of the year when hail is, in fact, more likely. Hailstones can cause great damage, and even fatal injuries.

Hailstorms happen when, in the vigorous air currents produced in a thunderous cumulonimbus cloud, small drops of water are swept upwards to regions of the cloud where the temperature is below freezing. There they form soft white ice crystal pellets, which enlarge until the air current can no longer support them. As they fall they pass through other supercooled raindrops that are still travelling upwards; these then freeze and surround the pellets with an opaque layer of white ice. As they fall through the lower part of the cloud, clear ice is added, forming balls that have been described as 'frozen gobstoppers'.

Sometimes hailstones get caught in another up-current, during which further layers of ice are added – possibly more than 20. This accounts for the massive size of some hailstones. The largest yet recorded, in Aurora, Nebraska, in June 2003, measured 178mm (7in) across.

> In an attempt to prevent hail church bells were rung and cannons fired, and medieval Christians erected so-called 'hail crosses' in fields to protect crops.

In the Bible, the Book of Joshua recounts the fate of the Canaanite army thus: 'As they fled from Israel down the pass, the Lord hurled great hailstones at them out of the sky all the way to Azekah, and they perished: more died from the hailstones than were slain by the swords of the Israelites.'

HAIL OF MANY SIZES

In 1986, the TORRO Hailstorm Intensity Scale was devised by Jonathan Webb of Oxford; TORRO is the acronym of Britain's Tornado and Storm Research Organization.

H0   Pea size, causes no damage.

H1   Leaves and flower petals punctured and torn.

H2   Leaves stripped from trees and plants.

H3   Panes of glass damaged, car bodywork dented.

H4   Some house windows broken; small tree branches broken off; birds killed.

H5   Many windows smashed; small animals injured; large tree branches broken off.

H6   Shingle roofs breached; metal roofs scored; wooden window frames broken away.

H7   Roofs shattered to expose rafters; cars seriously damaged.

H8   Shingle and tile roofs destroyed; small tree trunks split; people seriously injured.

H9   Concrete roofs broken; large tree trunks split and knocked down; people at risk of fatal injuries.

H10 Brick houses damaged; people at risk of fatal injuries.

A GREEN CLOUD IS A THUNDERCLOUD

A saying that comes from observing the colours of clouds before thunderstorms or even tornadoes, when light of unusual colour can sometimes be seen. The phenomenon has been used to dramatic effect on screen.

The reason why such bright colours – green-blue, yellow-green and even orange – appear in thunderclouds is not known, but meteorologists speculate that it may be due to the light-scattering effect of the huge amounts of water they hold. The effect seems to be most intense at sunset, as this 1848 account, written in the Pacific Ocean by a Captain Duncan on board the ship *Duke of Wellington*, records: 'At sunset we had a beautiful sky to the Westward; light hazy clouds shaded from light crimson to the lightest pink, with streaks of green between them; near the horizon the green was a very deep colour. My passengers were all admiring it, I told them that old sailors said that green in the sky betokened no good, and so it proved with us.'

The Sailor's Horn Book for the Law of Storms of 1876 includes a description from a Captain Jones of the barque *West* of an approaching cyclone in the South Indian Ocean, this time at the beginning of the day: 'Towards

sunrise blowing very hard, &c. A heavy black bank of clouds at N.E. which had wooden looking tops, and between the breaks in the bank appeared tinged with an orange colour. *They were very green'.*

Just less than a century later, on 3 and 4 April 1974, green thunderclouds were seen preceding the 'swarm' of 148 tornadoes that struck the American heartland and Ontario in Canada. At one point during the outbreak, 15 twisters were on the ground at the same time. One was on the ground for more than two hours.

LIGHTNING NEVER STRIKES TWICE IN THE SAME PLACE

Proverbially this observation has to do with misfortune and its recurrence, but it is a fallacy weatherwise. Lightning can even strike upwards – and is also reputed to leave its mark on anyone who witnesses it striking at close hand.

Statistically, the taller a structure the more likely it is to be hit more than once. On average, a two-storey building may be hit once in 100 years, but because lightning tends to strike the tallest object in the area, a building 450m (1,500ft) or higher may receive up to 20 hits in a year. In Peterborough, in May 2003, the tip of a golfer's umbrella was hit twice within half an hour. He lived to tell the tale.

Intense electrical fields above thunderstorms can create lightning that shoots upwards from thunderclouds, creating effects such as giant red blobs, puffs of blue light and even orange bursts that look like jellyfish as they explode into the sky. Such phenomena are called 'sprites'. In even rarer instances, exploding discs of light known as 'elves' may occur in the upper atmosphere.

Since medieval times, people have reported seeing 'lightning pictures' of struck objects on their bodies. Famously, a storm in Wells in Somerset in 1596 is believed to have imprinted the sign of the cross on members of the cathedral congregation, when lightning tore through the east end of the building.

The use of metal conductors arose from the proof by Benjamin Franklin that lightning was a form of electricity. He flew a kite with a metal key attached into a thundercloud and showed that the kite had become electrified.

LIGHTNING LORE

The appearance of lightning is believed to predict the weather, as reflected in these sayings:

Lightning in summer indicates good healthy weather.

Lightning without thunder after a clear day, there will be a continuance of fair weather.

If there be sheet lightning with a clear sky on spring, summer and autumn evenings, expect heavy rains.

And, according to the Chinese, the direction of lightning is also relevant:

With lightning in the east, the sun will be red;
With lightning in the west, showers you may dread;
With lightning in the south, it will rain more and more;
With lightning in the north, the southern gale will roar.

An April flood carries away the frog and her brood

And more besides. Spring floods are damaging to many animals and their young, especially those that live in watery habitats. Annual floods are, however, crucial to fertility in some areas of the world, such as the Nile Valley.

> The site at which frogs spawn is believed to indicate the weather to come. If they spawn in the middle of ponds then the summer will be hot and dry; if they choose the sides, wet weather is forecast.

By April, frogspawn will have hatched into a multitude of tadpoles, which will have little chance of developing into adult frogs if washed away by a flood. Toads and their tadpoles are equally vulnerable. Spring floods likely to be damaging to frogs happen when there is so much rain that rivers become swollen and overflow their banks as water rages downstream, destroying everything in its path. In shallow river valleys, water meadows were created from the Middle Ages, and possibly earlier. These not only acted as reservoirs for excess water but were deliberately flooded between November and early spring to produce high quality grass for grazing sheep.

The prosperity of ancient Egypt was directly related to the regular flooding of the Nile in late summer and early autumn. As the floods subsided they left behind an extremely fertile, alluvial soil, which allowed agriculture to flourish. The Nile god Hapi was believed to sit in a cave at Aswan, guarded by serpents, from where he poured the annual floodwaters from a bottomless jar.

TWO FULL MOONS IN A MONTH ARE SURE TO BRING FLOODS

The second full moon of the month is the proverbial 'blue moon', and the association with flooding arises from the notion that the heaviest rain follows the full moon, though this does not stand up to statistical scrutiny. A literally blue moon is another phenomenon that has been recorded.

Because of the way the calendar works, and because the full moon occurs every 28 days, the 'extra' days accumulate so that every two or three years there is a calendar month in which there are two full moons. This was once known as a 'betrayer moon' when it occurred early in the year during the season of Lent, because it would make the season come too early and induce hens to lay their eggs prematurely. Four or five times a century there are two blue moons in any one year: in 1999 they occurred in both January and March – there was no full moon in February. The phrase 'once in a blue moon' has come to mean something that occurs only rarely.

The moon can sometimes literally appear blue because of the effect of ash particles in the atmosphere that are just the right size to scatter red, but not blue light. The bluest moons yet recorded followed the eruption of Krakatoa in 1883 and forest fires in Alberta, Canada, in 1950.

MOON MYTHS

Each phase of the moon's cycle was once associated with a different deity:

HECATE – the moon before it has risen. The three-headed Greek goddess had powers over the heavens, land and sea.

ASTARTE – the crescent moon. The supreme fertility goddess of the Phoenicians.

DIANA – the moon in the open vault of the heavens. The Roman goddess of the hunt and the moon 'seated in her silver chair'.

SELENE – moonlight on the fields. This Greek goddess was the lover of the mortal shepherd's son Endymion, whom Zeus, at her request, cast into an eternal sleep so that he would always retain his youth and beauty.

OUT OF THE SOUTH COMETH THE WHIRLWIND

A Biblical quotation from the book of Job extolling the powers of the Almighty. However, it is also a comment on the weather of the Middle East, in which storms certainly do arise from a southerly direction.

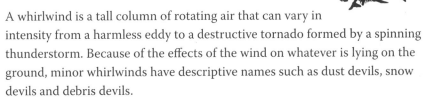

A whirlwind is a tall column of rotating air that can vary in intensity from a harmless eddy to a destructive tornado formed by a spinning thunderstorm. Because of the effects of the wind on whatever is lying on the ground, minor whirlwinds have descriptive names such as dust devils, snow devils and debris devils.

A whirlwind can take just a few seconds to form. Describing the tornado in Delphos, Ohio, on 30 May 1879, this account conjures up its sheer force: 'The cloud from which the funnel depended, seen at a distance of eight miles, appeared to be in terrible commotion; in fact while the hail was falling, a sort of tumbling in the clouds was noticed as they came up from the north-west and south-west, and about where they appeared to meet was the point at which the funnel was seen to descend. There was but one funnel at first, which was soon accompanied by several smaller ones, dangling down from the overhanging clouds like whip-lashes, and for some minutes they were appearing and disappearing like fairies at a play. Finally one of them seemed to expand and extend downwards more steadily than the others, resulting at length in what appeared to be their complete absorption.'

> To mitigate the effects of a whirlwind it is customary in some parts of America to throw dirt or water into them, or to clap the hands and stamp the feet.

Before a storm the sea heaves and sighs

This is certainly one of the effects of the wind on the sea as it puffs up the waves, and it is a warning to both sailors and fishermen. At the extremes of weather, the heaving sea may even transform itself into a waterspout.

The waterspout is a kind of tornado, though it can be weaker than its counterpart on land. As a wind funnel passing over water reaches a speed of about 64km/h (40mph) it sucks up a vortex of water. The point where it begins can often be seen as a black spot on the ocean or large lake. Waterspouts occur most frequently in the warm waters off the Florida coast.

The waterspout was one of the many dangers of the sea recognized and recorded by Pliny in his *Natural History*, although his remedy does not stand up to scrutiny: 'Cyclones,' he says, 'are particularly disastrous for sailors, as they twist round and shatter not only the yard-arms but also the ships. The only remedy, and this is a slight one, is to pour out vinegar before its approach, this substance being naturally cold. The whirlwind, when driven back by its own impact, snatches things up, carries them to the sky and sucks them aloft.'

Monsters of the deep were commonly regarded as responsible for the creation of storms at sea. Spenser uses this notion in *The Faerie Queen*, describing a wounded dragon:

He cryde, as raging seas are wont to rore,
When wintry storme his wrathfull wreck does threat,
The rolling billowes beat the ragged shore,
As they the earth would shoulder from her seat,
And greedie gulfe does gape, as he would eat
His neighbour element in his revenge:
Then gin the blustring brethren boldly threat,
To move the world from off his stedfast henge,
And boystrous battell make, each other to avenge.

Having a clergyman on board ship is thought to bring bad weather at sea because while ministers may tame the Devil on land, it is the Devil who has the upper hand on the ocean.

WITH COMETS COME CALAMITIES

A saying that harks back to the ancient, deep-seated fear of comets and the effects that these 'blazing stars' were believed to have, not merely on the weather but on the fates of humans and even the course of history.

In his *Contemplation of Mysteries* of 1571, Thomas Hill listed the many disasters that a comet might bring: 'Drought, the pestilence, hunger, battles, the alteration of kingdoms, and common weales, and the traditions of men.

Also winds, earthquakes, dearth, landfloods, and great heat to follow.' And earlier, in the third century BC, the *Phaenomena* of Aratus had included this dire prediction:

> *No grateful sight to husbandmen appear*
> *One or more comets, with their blazing hair,*
> *Forerunners of a parched and barren year.*

Comets, described by Aristotle as 'stars with hair', are small star-like bodies made of ice, dust and rock, which orbit the sun. When visible from earth, most have glowing 'tails'. Describing one seen by the Egyptians, and named for Typhon, 'the king at the time', Pliny says: 'The comet was fiery in appearance and twisted after the manner of a coil; it looked wild and was not really a star so much as a kind of ball of fire.' The detail of the comet's form was once also considered relevant. In the sixth century Gregory of Tours writes, in his *De cursu stellarum*: 'When a comet seem to have a flaming diadem, it portends the death of a king. When it has a long ray like a sword, glowing red, and spreads its hair abroad darkly it announces ruin to the country.'

Because of their massive elliptical orbits, comets appear and reappear at long but regular intervals. The most famous of all is Halley's comet – named for the English astronomer Edmond Halley, who calculated its orbit in 1705 – which can be seen approximately every 75 years.

As to portents, it was almost certainly coincidence that the appearance of Halley's comet preceded the death of the Roman Emperor Macrinus in the year AD 218 and Attila's only defeat in battle in 451. In 1066, the comet was regarded in England as a warning of the Norman Conquest; it is depicted in the Bayeux tapestry, with frightened people pointing to it and others bringing news of the omen to the newly crowned King Harold.

Even though they may have no effect on the weather, in weather lore comets are linked with cold conditions. In France they are said to improve the grape crop, and wine produced in years when they appear is dubbed 'comet wine'.

Storms are witches' work

It has long been believed that witches have the power to raise storms in order to wreck ships and destroy crops. The ways in which they are alleged to operate are many and various.

In times past, whenever damage was caused by a storm the blame was laid at the doors of witches – because, like sorcerers, they were possessed of the wherewithal to control the elements. In his *Compendium Maleficarum* ('Handbook of Witches') of 1626, the Italian friar Francesco Maria Guazzo, writing at the behest of the Bishop of Milan to publicize the evils of witches, said: 'Witches have confessed that they made hailstorms on the sabat, or whenever they wished, to blast the fruits of the earth. To this end, according to their confession, they beat water with a wand, and then they threw into the air or into the water a certain powder which Satan had given them. By this means, a cloud was raised which afterwards turned to hailstones and fell wherever the witches wished. When water was lacking,' he concluded, 'they used their urine.'

Other methods of storm-raising, supposed to be equally effective, included shaking a wet broom, throwing pieces of flint over the left shoulder, boiling hog bristles – or even babies – in the witches' cauldrons, laying sticks on a dry river bank, or burying sage leaves and allowing them to rot. In Scotland, at their trial in 1662, the Auldearn witches were

> *It was said that a storm would arise when a witch died, this being a sign that the Devil had been alerted to claim back one of his own.*

accused of using a wet rag to beat a so-called 'cursing stone' while reciting the following spell three times:

I knock this rag upon this stone,
To raise the wind in the Devil's name,
It shall not lie until I please again.

Sailors were particularly wary of the storm-raising wiles of witches, but tried to ensure good weather by giving them money. In return the witch would give the sailor a length of knotted cord. When at sea, untying one of the knots would raise a favourable breeze.

MEN MAY WHISTLE UP A BREEZE

In the days of sail, sailors used this old way to try to raise a wind when they were faced with the dead calm of the doldrums. However, whistling was an activity that needed to be engaged in with extreme caution.

The doldrums, also known as equatorial calms, occur in areas of the Atlantic, Pacific and Indian oceans, in a low-pressure belt known as the intertropical convergence zone. Before the advent of steam the doldrums could keep ships becalmed for weeks on end, as they do yachts today. However, as well

In the 19th century, the word 'doldrum' referred to a dullard – that is, a dull or sluggish person. It probably derived from 'dol', or 'dull', given the same form as the word 'tantrum'. So while a tantrum was a fit of temper, a doldrum was one of sloth and dullness, or a person behaving in such a way.

as producing very light winds, the effect of heat rising from the region can also trigger squalls, thunderstorms and even hurricanes.

At sea, whistling is allowed only in extreme circumstances, because if you make a sound like a distant gale it is thought that a gale will surely arrive. If it should be essential to whistle up a breeze it must be done only by the ship's master, and only when he is facing in the direction from which he wants the wind to come. On land, women – and especially the wives of fishermen – were warned against whistling up winds that might come from the wrong direction and so put their husbands and other men in jeopardy.

In his poem 'The Rime of the Ancient Mariner', Samuel Taylor Coleridge vividly describes the plight of a ship's crew trapped in the doldrums:

All in a hot and copper sky,
The bloody Sun, at noon
Right up above the mast did stand,
No bigger than the Moon.

Day after day, day after day,
We stuck, nor breath nor motion;
As idle as a painted ship
Upon a painted ocean.

A WINTER FOG WILL FREEZE A DOG

In winter freezing fog can linger near the ground and can play tricks on the eyes. Most notorious of all fogs were London's 'pea soupers', which could have fatal effects.

Dense winter fog is effectively a very low cloud created when cold, wet, stagnant air lingers near the ground. It is most likely to form around dawn, when the air temperature has fallen consistently for several hours. In such a fog, it is very easy, especially for drivers, to lose all sense of speed and distance. Equally, small objects can appear huge. This so-called 'fog loom' was described by Leonardo da Vinci in his *Treatise on Painting*, who experienced it in Milan. 'There is great deception,' he wrote '. . . the eye being accustomed to see an object diminished in size at a great distance supposes this to be farther off than it is, and consequently imagines it larger.'

London's 'pea-soupers' began in the 13th century, when cheap sea coal from the north-east became available for heating homes. Water vapour condensed around soot particles in the air, leading to smog, which John Evelyn described in *Fumifugium*, his anti-coal treatise of 1661, as 'thick Mist accompanied with a fuliginous and filthy vapour', which would last for days on end. As well as precipitating deaths from bronchitis, smogs were extremely disruptive. One 'fog monitor' of 1902 wrote: 'White and damp in the early morning, it became smoky later, the particles coated with soot being dry and pungent to inhale. There was a complete block of the street traffic at some crossings. Omnibuses were abandoned, and several goods trains were taken off.'

In December 1952 a four-day smog killed at least 4,000 Londoners, following which pressure mounted for legislation. With the passing of the Clean Air Act in 1956, sulphur dioxide pollution decreased and smogs became increasingly rare.

Winds in Conflict Bring on Hurricanes

An old saying whose accuracy is not borne out by modern science. Hurricanes are much to be feared for the havoc the winds within them can wreak.

That the 'hurricane season' lasts from around August until November relates closely to the water temperature needed to trigger it. A hurricane forms when, in tropical seas, the water is warmer than 26.5°C (80°F); the adjacent air is heated and rises, creating an area of low pressure. As moisture in the air accumulates, thunderclouds form and the air begins to spin as the warm air rises, forming a central vortex or 'eye'. As the hurricane moves, it is likely – as in the Gulf of Mexico – to hit land. Here, deprived of moisture from the sea, it cools and dissipates, but not before it has done its damage.

On 29 August 2005 hurricane Katrina hit the coast of Louisiana with winds blowing at about 200km/h (125mph). The winds whipped up the sea, creating a surge about 10m (33ft) high, which fractured the levees of New Orleans and flooded some 80 per cent of the city. At least 1,830 people lost their lives, and the cost of the damage was estimated at nearly $100 billion.

Each hurricane is designated a name. For several hundred years, hurricanes in the West Indies were often named after the particular saint's day on which they occurred, such as Hurricane San Felipe, which struck Puerto Rico on 13 September 1876. Using women's names became the practice during World War II, following the use of the name 'Maria' for the hurricane in George R. Stewart's 1941 novel *Storm*. In 1951 the

The remnants of 'dead' Atlantic hurricanes can strike the British Isles, and it was probably one of these that caused the infamous storm that hit southern Britain in October 1987.

USA adopted a confusing plan to name storms by a phonetic alphabet (Able, Baker, Charlie . . .), but in 1953 the nation's weather services returned to using female names. This practice ended in 1978, when names from both genders were chosen to designate storms in the eastern Pacific. A year later, male and female names were included in lists for the Atlantic and Gulf of Mexico. In creating the lists of names, the initials Q, U, X, Y, and Z are not included because of the scarcity of names beginning with them. Equally, names associated with storms that have caused significant death and damage are usually retired from the list.

THERE IS LIGHTNING LIGHTLY BEFORE THUNDER

The confirmation, in a 16th-century proverb, that unless a storm is directly overhead lightning is seen before a thunderclap is heard. Timing the gap between the two makes it possible to calculate the distance of a storm.

While lightning is an electrical discharge, thunder is a sound effect created as air is heated and waves set in motion as a result of this electrical activity. These waves travel at about 300m (1,000ft) per second but do not always sound the same. Sometimes they are heard as low rumbles, at others as sharp, sinister crashes. However it is rare to hear thunder from more than 16km (10 miles) away.

In many cultures links are made between birds and thunder. The thunderbirds of Native American mythology are creatures with supernatural powers, which, as well as producing storms, are responsible for both war and peace. In the Crow Indian tradition, the thunderbird wears a cloak of eagle feathers and creates thunder by flapping its wings. Lightning occurs when it opens or shuts its eyes, or uses its claws to rip open trees to locate the grubs that are its favourite food.

> *To avert thunder and lightning it was traditional to plant houseleeks (Sempervivum tectorum) on roofs, these being plants sacred to Jupiter, the Roman thunder god.*

HOW FAR AWAY?

In *The Weather Eye*, published in 1940, C.R. Benstead analysed the timing of a peal of thunder. Each 'branch' is a part of the discharge of the storm:

Time

0 sec – Flash seen by observer.

8 sec – Roll begins and thereby shows that the nearest branch was about 1½ miles [2.5km] away.

15 sec – Claps begin and thereby show that the next branch was about 3 miles [5km] away.

25 sec – Claps cease and thereby indicate that the most distant branch was about 5 miles [8km] away.

35 sec – Roll ends.

Beware a ball of fire

Or in other words, be very wary of St Elmo's fire, a phenomenon created during thunderstorms and regarded with particular suspicion – and caution – by sailors.

When, during a storm, the air reaches an extremely high voltage, a large electrical charge builds up around pointed objects such as the masts of ships. This creates a light effect – a ball of fire that looks like real flames.

The appearance of St Elmo's fire could also presage a storm, as Longfellow correctly observes in *The Golden Legend*:

> *Last night I saw St Elmo's stars,*
> *With their glimmering lanterns, all at play*
> *On the tops of the masts and the tips of the spars,*
> *And I knew we should have foul weather today.*

'St Elmo' is an alternative name for St Erasmus, a fourth-century martyr who became the patron saint of seamen. He was said to have continued preaching when lightning struck the ground beside him, and sailors took St Elmo's fire as a sign of his protection. Its alternative name, 'corposant', comes from the Portuguese *corpo santo*, meaning 'holy body'.

The Romans related the phenomenon to the twin deities Castor and Pollux, who were also revered as the patrons of sailors. The number of balls of fire and their behaviour were significant. Pliny (as interpreted by Francis Bacon) says: 'The ball of fire called Castor by the ancients, that appears at sea, if it be single, prognosticates a severe storm . . . which will be much more severe if the ball does not adhere to the mast, but rolls or dances about. But if there are two of them . . . and that, too, when the storm

St Elmo's fire may be the origin of the legend of the Flying Dutchman, *the phantom ship surrounded by ghostly blue light seen off the Cape of Good Hope.*

has increased, it is reckoned a good sign. But if there are three of them . . . the storm will soon become more fearful.'

THE MONSOON ARRIVES IN JUNE

Or sometimes in late May – at least in Asia. This regular spell of intensely rainy weather is a feature of the Asian climate whose causes were first worked out by the astronomer Edmond Halley, although his explanation has recently been challenged and updated.

According to Halley's theory, first proposed during his voyage in 1676 to the South Atlantic and developed in the following centuries, the monsoon arises from a kind of massive sea breeze. The sun heats the earth more at the equator than in other regions. The hot air that rises over the land contrasts with the cooler moisture-filled air rising from the

The word monsoon comes from the Arabic word mausim *meaning 'season'.*

sea. The resulting pressure differences lead to the formation of strong south-westerly winds, which blow inland and, as they do so, trigger heavy rainfall. As the land cools down the process is reversed, the wind becomes north-easterly and the rain dries up.

The most modern theory, put forward by geoscientists at the California Institute of Technology and based on computer modelling, proposes that monsoons arise as a result of an interaction between tropical circulation and large-scale turbulent eddies generated in middle latitudes, which 'crash' into one another. As they 'break', rather like waves on a beach, they make the wind change very rapidly.

> In World War II the arrival of the monsoon, which cut off Japanese supplies to Kohima in Burma, was instrumental in helping the Allies defeat the invaders.

India and Sri Lanka rely totally on the arrival of monsoon rains to ensure the harvests. Of all the locations in the subcontinent, Trivandrum on the southern tip of India is most consistent in that the monsoon arrives there each year on 1 June. In the tropical northern regions of Australia the monsoon season begins in January, while in Arizona September is 'monsoon month'.

THE STARS FALL AS A FOUL JELLY

The foul-smelling gelatinous substance that occasionally falls to earth, sometimes during rainstorms, is as yet unexplained. It may possibly emanate from meteor showers, or may have a more mundane origin.

'Star jelly', also called *pwdre sêr* from the Welsh meaning 'rot of the stars', has been recorded at various times for many centuries. The scientist Robert Boyle recorded in 1661 that he had seen 'a good quantity of that jelly, that is sometimes found on the ground'. Twenty years before, Sir John Suckling penned the lines:

> *As he, whose quicker eye doth trace*
> *A false star shot to a mark'd place,*
> *Does run apace,*
> *And thinking it to catch,*
> *A jelly up does snatch.*

And in his novel *The Talisman* of 1825 Sir Walter Scott writes: ' "Seek a falling star," said the hermit, "and thou shalt only light on some foul jelly, which, in shooting through the horizon, has assumed for a moment an appearance of splendour." '

The link with meteors comes from observations such as that of a Mrs Sybil Christian of Frisco, Texas, who discovered several blobs of purple goo on 11 August 1979 following a Perseid meteor shower. On 23 June 1978, Mrs Ephgrave of Cambridge saw a ball of white jelly about the size of a football fall to the ground during a heavy rainstorm. She was able to prod it, and found that it stayed intact, but it had completely disappeared by the following morning.

Other explanations of star jelly propose that it is frogspawn regurgitated by birds, remains of frogs and toads or even some kind of blue-green alga.

Star jelly is supposed to have inspired the 1958 film *The Blob* starring Steve McQueen. The plot centres on a gelatinous ball that falls from space on a shooting star and consumes everything in its path as it grows and grows.

THE WORST WEATHER, RAINING CATS AND DOGS

Or even fish, frogs or crabs. Heavy rain can affect all manner of animal life, and falls of various creatures from the sky have long been documented.

It was in 1653 that the expression 'It shall raine . . . dogs and polecats' was first recorded, but there is no one unequivocal explanation. One theory is that it relates to the fact that in Norse weather lore the cat was supposed to have great influence on the weather and to have 'a gale of wind in her tail'. Another is that the saying originates from the Greek word *catadupa*, meaning 'waterfall' or 'cataract'. More likely is that cats and dogs were drowned in poorly drained medieval streets during severe storms. This last explanation is given weight by Jonathan Swift's 'Description of a City Shower' of 1710:

> *Now, from all parts the swelling kennels flow*
> *And bear their trophies with them as they go . . .*
> *Drowned puppies, stinking sprats, all drench'd in mud*
> *Dead cats and turnip-tops come tumbling down the flood.*

Freak falls of fish and other animals probably arise when tornadoes suck up water from lakes and even the sea and carry the creatures aloft. Since they are too heavy to be held for any length of time they then fall to the ground. One of the largest 'fish falls' recorded was in 1859 at Mountain Ash in Wales, but as recently as 2004 a shower of 19 crabs fell into a garden in Dartford, Kent.

Untimely storms make men expect a dearth

A quotation from Shakespeare's *Richard III* expressing fear at the effects sudden changes in the weather might have on crops and livelihoods. The two worst storms on record in Britain happened in 1703 and 1987.

The Great Storm of 1703 began on 24 November. Over 8,000 sailors lost their lives as ships were smashed on to the rocks, while the then newly constructed Eddystone Lighthouse, on the border between Devon and Cornwall, was entirely destroyed – together with its architect Henry Winstanley – by the storm. Countless farm animals were drowned, notably when water surged up the Severn Estuary. In the New Forest alone 4,000 oak trees were felled.

The event led Daniel Defoe to produce his first book, *The Storm*, published in July 1704. 'No pen,' he wrote, 'could describe it, nor tongue express it, nor thought conceive it unless by one in the extremity of it . . .'. He described the destruction of forests all over England; Portsmouth and other coastal towns 'looked as if the enemy had sackt them and were most miserably torn to pieces'. He also recorded 700 vessels grounded in the Thames between Limehouse and Shadwell.

On the night of 15 October 1987, Britain's weather forecasters were notoriously adrift, predicting heavy rain rather than wind. By the end of the next day 15 million trees had fallen, including six of the seven famous oak trees at

Sevenoaks in Kent, and 18 people had lost their lives. As the storm hit the Isle of Wight at 2.00 am, Shanklin Pier was broken into three pieces by mountainous waves. Although it was not, technically, a hurricane, the winds recorded had a force equivalent to a Category 1 hurricane.

END A DROUGHT – THROW WATER ON STONE

One of very many old ways believed to help bring on much-needed rain, often accompanied by the recital of incantations. Other rituals used to help induce precipitation include processions and rain dances.

Droughts are usually the result of prevalent high-pressure systems and winds blowing from landmasses rather than off the sea, from where they gather water vapour. Britain's last drought was that of the summer of 1976, when parts of the south-west were without rain for 45 days during July and August. In world terms, oceanic and atmospheric

The need for dry weather for the harvest is expressed in the saying, 'Dry August and warm does the harvest no harm.'

weather cycles such as El Niño-Southern Oscillation are also relevant, and are responsible for making droughts a regular occurrence along the Pacific coast of the Americas and Australia.

Everywhere in the world, and throughout the ages, people have developed different ways of making it rain. For the ancient Greeks, propitiating the sky god Zeus was the key to success. A branch of oak (his sacred tree) was dipped in water while prayers were offered. In medieval times, images of saints were dipped in water during a drought; as well as being a kind of magical rite, this was regarded as a punishment for their refusal to answer people's prayers.

In North America, the Cherokee are among the native peoples known to perform rain dances, serving the dual purpose of bringing rain and cleansing the earth of evil spirits. Feathers and blue clothing are worn, to symbolize wind and rain. The Aymara of South America still adhere to the ancient rite in which a shaman or *paqo* rows out into Lake Titicaca and, having filled basins with water, frogs and water plants, leaves offerings to the spirits of the deep. The basins are taken to the top of a mountain called Atoja and placed on altars dedicated to the sun. The *paqo* then prays to the mountain spirits for rain. As the heat evaporates the water in the basins, the cries of the frogs ring out and the gods, in their pity for the thirsty creatures, send rain.

Any rain is welcome to end a drought, but according to the old saying:

Rain from the south prevents the drought;
But rain from the west is always best.

The reason is that rain from the west is likely to be heavier and longer lasting.

Modern science is able to 'make' rain by 'seeding' or adding particles to clouds. The process was discovered in July 1946 by the American chemist and meteorologist Vincent Schaefer when using dry ice to lower the temperature of his deep freeze. The result was a haze of ice crystals, which in clouds are the forerunners of rain.

CHAPTER 6

FEAST AND
FESTIVAL

S ayings that predict or comment on the weather at particular times of year regularly make reference to saints' days or church festivals. And with good reason, for in the days before mass education and communication these were the dates that punctuated the seasons of the year. As well as being times for particular observation – or celebration – some of these dates were the occasions for specific activities and events. St Michael's Day or Michaelmas, 29 September, for instance, was the date when farm tenancies were renewed (and in many cases still are) while Lammas, 1 August, was a time for offering up the first fruits of the harvest. Despite the somewhat mythological nature of many of the sayings in this chapter they serve to keep us in touch with the ways of the past and the history of our saints and celebrations.

Some saints, notably St Swithin and St Valentine, were once believed to have divine powers of weather prediction, but in fact are no more reliable than the behaviour of the North American groundhog – or in Britain creatures such as the badger – which, at Candlemas (2 February), will forecast either an early spring or the continuation of winter. Another reason to doubt the accuracy of many of these traditional forecasts is that they date from before the change of the British calendar in 1752, when the days between 3–13 September were cut from the year by Act of Parliament to correct a discrepancy in timekeeping.

ALL WHITE AND STILL THE NEW YEAR LIES

But not necessarily. As well as making resolutions, New Year is traditionally a time for predicting the weather for the coming months.

There are many reasons for taking note of the weather at the turn of the year, according to the old verse:

If New Year's Eve night wind blow south,
It betokeneth warmth and growth;
If west, much milk and fish in the sea;
If north, much cold and storms there will be;
If east, the trees will bear much fruit;
If north-east, flee it man and brute.

In fact, these are more likely to be short-term than long-term predictions. And the weather can be extremely changeable, as this diary entry for 1 January from *Old Days in Country Places* (c. 1923) confirms: 'Yesterday awoke to a blue sky, and here and there over it soft brown and grey clouds, tender as the colours on a wood-pigeon's breast and as beautiful. But it was a misleading tenderness. Before the light was two hours old the heavens were black with clouds, and there came a storm of wild wind and rain . . . This morning was frosty. In a blue sky, flecked by pink clouds, a cherry-coloured sun rose, and as it climbed higher there came a mysterious light on the trees to the west, revealing the filmy brown bloom of seed cases on the bare boughs. The year had turned.'

As to New Year weather predictions, Scotland has one of the most complex, as recorded by Thomas Pennant in 1772: 'The Highlanders form a sort of almanack, or presage of the weather of the ensuing year, in the following manner: They make observation on twelve days, beginning the last of December; and hold as an infallible rule, that whatsoever weather happens on each of those days, the same will prove to agree in the corresponding months. Thus, January is to answer to the weather of December 31st, February to that of January 1st, and so with the rest. Old people,' he adds, 'still pay great attention to this augury.'

St Hilary is the coldest day of the year

This could be 13 or 14 January, since both have been used for the feast of St Hilary, but there is no doubt that it often coincides with a plunging of the thermometer.

One of the most severe winters in history began around 13 January 1205, when the Thames in London froze over, and ale and wine turned to solid ice and were consequently sold by weight rather than volume. Similarly, in his *Chronicles* of 1567, the English historian John Stow recorded: 'So began a frost which continued till the two and twentieth day of March, so that the ground could not be tilled; whereof it came to pass that, in summer following a quarter of wheat was sold for a mark of silver in many places of England, which for the more part in the

days of King Henry the Second was sold for twelve pence; a quarter of beans or peas for half a mark; a quarter of oats for thirty pence, that were wont to be sold for fourpence.'

Centuries later, writers were still bemoaning the cold. Writing in Paris on 14 January 1689, Madame de Sévigné records: 'The cold is excessive; our thermometer is as low as it can go, our river is frozen; it snows, it freezes and freezes again at the same time; nobody can keep their footing in the streets: I stay at home and sit in the Chevalier's room.'

The coldest day of the year in Britain usually occurs after the shortest day, because the sea continues to cool until well into January. During late December, although the sun is at its weakest, there is still enough warmth in the sea to fend off the worst of the cold. But once winds surge down from the Arctic in the early months of the year, icy weather sets in.

If St Paul's Day be fair and clear, it doth betide a happy year

These are the first lines of a verse of prognostication by the 17th-century astrologer and almanac-maker William Lilly. The feast of the conversion of St Paul, which falls on 25 January, is held to be significant for weather predictions in many European countries.

The verse in full runs thus:

If St Paul's Day be fair and clear,
It doth betide a happy year;
But if by chance it then should rain,
It will make dear all kinds of grain;
And if the clouds make dark the sky,
Then neat [cattle] and fowls this year shall die;
If blustering winds do blow aloft,
Then wars shall vex the realm full oft.

In times past, as today, dry weather at the end of January was undoubtedly welcome in the middle of a wet winter, but the saying is less apt nowadays, since winter droughts have become considerably more common in recent years. Equally, in the days before advances in veterinary medicine made it possible to treat diseases of cattle and other livestock, and before cattle were brought indoors during the cold months, warm wet weather would undoubtedly have decreased their likelihood of surviving the winter.

In France, and in Denmark and other Scandinavian countries, St Paul's Day was also believed to predict the weather for the coming seasons. In Norway it was officially recorded as 'fair' as long as the sun shone long enough for a farmer to harness and unharness a horse three times, or if the rain held off long enough for the rider to mount and dismount.

In the Christian calendar, the conversion of the Jew Saul of Tarsus when he experienced a vision of Christ on the road to Damascus is not a date that is marked with any great celebration, despite Paul's central place in the teaching of the Church. It is possible that the date was originally observed to mark the removal of his remains from the place of his martyrdom in Rome (believed to be in AD 36) to their final resting place in the city.

> The last 12 days of January, which include St Paul's Day, are said in country lore to rule the weather for the rest of the year.

THE SHEPHERD WOULD RATHER SEE THE WOLF ENTER HIS FOLD ON CANDLEMAS THAN THE SUN

For the reason that sunshine on Candlemas Day, 2 February – a date long associated with predicting the arrival of spring – is believed to signal that six weeks of winter are yet to come. In America it is known as Groundhog Day.

Candlemas, which is 40 days after Christmas, is the Christian feast of the Purification of the Virgin Mary. The roots of the festival go back to at least the sixth century, when this date was taken to be the middle of winter and the point after which the sun's strength rapidly begins to intensify. On Candlemas Eve, also the feast of St Brigid, it was customary to make new effigies of the saint out of wheat or oats (and to burn the old ones) to ensure crop fertility, and for a young woman to carry flowers into the home.

Among the many weather predictions for Candlemas is this verse:

> *If Candlemas Day be fair and bright,*
> *Winter will have another flight,*
> *But if Candlemas Day be clouds and rain,*
> *Winter is gone and will not come again.*

The truth is that the weather in February and even in March is very fickle and almost impossible to predict.

As far as wildlife is concerned, the bear and badger may make brief exits from hibernation at this time, but the groundhog has been inextricably linked with Candlemas since 1886, when Clymer Freas, then editor of the western Pennsylvania newspaper *The Punxsutawney Spirit*, reported that, because the groundhog had emerged from his den – but not seen his shadow – that day, there would be an early spring. Conversely, the emerging animal that witnesses its shadow predicts another six weeks of winter. While the groundhog's forays are probably more to do with prospecting for mates than predicting the weather, the day has more than retained its newsworthiness.

MORE CANDLEMAS PREDICTIONS

The idea that Candlemas weather will be the opposite of that to come is preserved in numerous traditional sayings:

As far as the sun shines on
    Candlemas Day,
So far will the snow blow before May.

If Candlemas Day be fine and clear,
Corn and fruits will then be dear.

If on February 2nd the goose find it wet,
the sheep will have grass on March 25th.

If it neither rains or snows on
    Candlemas Day,
You may straddle your horse and go
    and buy hay.

As long before Candlemas as the lark is heard to sing, so long will he be silent afterwards on account of the cold.

Never come Lent, never come winter

Lent usually begins in February, a month noted for its continued wintry weather. Yet February also reveals the first signs of spring, as birds begin to tune their voices.

In Britain cold spells of weather are common in early February, and are associated with high pressure over Greenland and the Arctic and low pressure over most of Europe. Cold days between 7 and 10 February are known as Buchan's first period, named for the Scottish amateur meteorologist Alexander Buchan (1829–1907), but the cold spell is unlikely to fall between such precise dates.

A diarist of the 1920s, writing in Herefordshire on 6 February, highlights the season's contrasts: 'Again winter. Rain and snow, but the little brown wren sang a short ditty as it crept about the hedge. In the afternoon the weather improved, and it was pleasant to see signs of returning spring once more – the fresh green leaves of the cuckoo-pint uncurling, the elders in leaf, and the cleavers already beginning to climb up the hedgerows.'

Lent gets its name from the Old English word *lencten* meaning 'spring' but also 'lengthening', because of the increasing hours of daylight. In the Christian calendar it commemorates the 40 days that Jesus spent in the wilderness before his return to Jerusalem and his crucifixion and resurrection. This period of frugality and fasting, following the making

> *'Lent lily' is another name for the wild daffodil (*Narcissus pseudonarcissus*), which blooms in March.*

of pancakes and the other celebrations of Shrove Tuesday (Mardi Gras), was instituted in the fourth century. Initially it lasted 36 days, and was not increased to 40 days until 300 years later.

Meat was once forbidden food during Lent and 'red herrings' – fish preserved by being dried and smoked until they were a deep brownish red – were common fare. Salt fish was also eaten, although Thomas Tusser had this recommendation for farmers in 1580:

> *Let Lent well kept, offend not thee,*
> *for March and April breeders be,*
> *Spend herring first, save saltfish last:*
> *for saltfish is good when Lent is past.*

To St Valentine, the spring is a neighbour

Because by 14 February the weather may be expected to be on the turn. And by the time of this festival for lovers, some flowers – the harbingers of spring – will be in bloom.

It is an old belief that by the middle of February 'winter's back breaks' and, as the days get longer, the weather begins to warm. Rain on and around Valentine's Day may or may not be welcomed, depending on what you believe.

According to Scottish Highland lore, the weather of 12–14 February is borrowed from January, and it is a good omen if these days are wet and stormy. However, according to a further rhyme:

> *If the last eighteen days of February be*
> *Wet, and the first ten days of March, you'll see*
> *That the spring quarter, and the summer too,*
> *Will prove too wet, and danger to ensue.*

The flowers that foretell the arrival of spring around mid-month include the snowdrop – the 'fair maid of February' – and the aconite. Praising the arrival of the latter, and the fact that its flowers do not persist into the spring, the 19th-century English poet Thomas Noel wrote:

> *Flower, that foretell'st a Spring thou ne'er shall see,*
> *Yet smilest still upon thy wintry day,*
> *Content with thy joy-giving destiny,*
> *Nor envying fairer flowers their festal May, –*
> *O golden-chaliced Aconite!*

St Valentine's Day was adopted by the makers of the Christian calendar from the bawdy fertility festival of Lupercalia. The date is also said to be when birds begin to mate. Historically, there were several St Valentines, but two with 14 February as their feast day. Both were Christian martyrs of the third century, one a Roman priest, the other a bishop of Terni in Umbria.

Long before it became customary to send red roses for St Valentine's Day, seeing gorse in bloom was a good sign because 'When gorse is out of bloom, kissing's out of fashion'. Luckily, gorse is nearly always in flower, but the saying also reflects the fact that it grows on heaths and commons, where lovers could meet away from the watchful eyes of their families.

Upon St David's Day, put Oats and Barley in the Clay

A timely instruction for farmers and gardeners to get on with sowing their seeds. The first day of March, which we celebrate as St David's Day, was the beginning of the Roman year.

As well as 1 March, the following day – the feast of St Chad – was believed to be good for sowing other crops:

> Sow peas and beans on David
>   and Chad
> Be the weather good or bad.
> If they're not in by Benedick
>   [21 March]
> They had better stop in the ricke.

Not all farmers would adhere to this instruction, however. In Devon, for example, the first three days of March were known as 'blind days' and were considered so unlucky that no farmer would risk sowing seeds then.

To celebrate the feast of St David, the patron saint of Wales, daffodils are worn, and also leeks. According to legend Welsh warriors, engaged in battle against the Saxons in the seventh century, wore leeks in their hats to show which side they were on. More prosaically, the leek may have been adopted simply because it is a vegetable that overwinters well and is still good to eat at this time of year.

> In ancient Rome, the start of the year was marked by processions and hymns and special attention to tending the fires of Vesta, goddess of hearth and home.

BEFORE ST CHAD EVERY GOOSE LAYS BOTH GOOD AND BAD

A reference to the laying habits of geese over the winter, prior to the feast day of St Chad on 2 March. Geese have long been prized for their tasty flesh and for their vigilance.

> *The cackling of a goose is said to predict rain. On the other hand:*
>
> If the wild geese gang [go] out to sea,
> Good weather there will surely be.

Traditionally, the arrival of the first goose eggs of the year coincides with St Valentine's Day, 14 February, but geese may lay sporadically over the winter months and it is also said that on Candlemas (2 February) 'the good goose begins to lay'. A domesticated goose will lay up to 160 eggs a year; bigger than hens' eggs, and with a larger, dense yolk, they are excellent to eat and make particularly good mayonnaise.

Geese are popular domestic birds because they demand little attention and will graze on grass and corn stubble, although they require additional food such as maize if they are to be fattened for the table. Their cackling also serves to warn of the approach of strangers. The goose is now a Christmas bird, but in country districts it was traditional to eat geese at Michaelmas, when they were plump, and again as young 'green geese' at Whitsun (Pentecost).

Look for the lady's smock on Lady Day

Except in a very warm spring, Lady Day on 25 March is now early for the flowering of this pretty plant, but would not have been before the calendar was changed in 1752.

In the Church calendar, 25 March is the Feast of the Annunciation of the Blessed Virgin, corresponding to the moment of Christ's conception.

The lady's smock (*Cardamine pratensis*), originally called 'our lady's smock' but also known as the cuckoo flower, meadow bittercress or milkmaids, thrives in marshes and damp meadows. Its common names come from the resemblance of its pale lilac blooms to a smock laid out to dry, from the fact that it flowers at about the time of the cuckoo's arrival and from the taste of its leaves, which were once valued as a salad.

Until Britain's change from the Julian to the Gregorian calendar in 1752, Lady Day fell on 6 April. This was the date when contracts such as those between tenant farmers and landowners were renewed or new ones begun, and it remains significant in Britain as the beginning of the tax year.

The delightful sight of lady's smock in flower was celebrated by Alfred Austin in 'A Spring Carol':

At first but single,
And then in flocks,
In dell and dingle,
The Lady-Smocks
Make mist for the golden cowslip tapers,
To shine like a sunrise through the morning vapours.

THE CHERRY WEARS THE WHITE OF EASTERTIDE

One of the many flowers of the season, the cherry blossom is a potent symbol of spring, especially for the Japanese. As at Christmas, the weather at Easter has long been believed to foretell what is to come in the weeks ahead.

The link between the cherry and Easter is celebrated in the poem 'Loveliest of Trees' by A.E. Housman, which begins:

> *Loveliest of trees, the cherry now*
> *Is hung with bloom along the bough,*
> *And stands about the woodland ride*
> *Wearing white for Eastertide.*

Weather watchers will take note of the weather on the days leading up to Easter, as well as the day itself. A bad year is forecast by poor weather on Palm Sunday, but rain on Good Friday is believed to foreshadow a fertile year. Easter being a movable feast that can fall from late March to the third week of April, the weather can vary from snow to warm sunshine, but in weather lore a late Easter is associated (unreliably) with a long, cold spring.

In Japan, the honouring of spring blossoms with the celebration called *hanami*

is a ritual that goes back centuries, though only since the Heian period (AD 794–1185) has cherry blossom been its focus (before that time it centred on the Japanese apricot). Each spring Japanese meteorologists report daily on the northward movement of the *sakura zensen*, or 'cherry blossom front', as the first blossoms open, and friends and families gather for picnics under the trees. The unpredictability of the blossom's arrival, and its fleeting nature, have led to the saying: 'If there were no cherry blossoms in this world, how much more tranquil our hearts would be in spring.'

EASTER WEATHER

. . . and what is to come. As ever, the old lore is full of contradictions:

Such weather as there is on Easter Day there will be at harvest – but a rainy Easter betokens slim fodder.

A good deal of rain upon Easter Day Gives a good crop of grass, but little good hay.

If there is fair weather from Easter to Whitsuntide, butter will be cheap [that is, the cows will produce plenty of milk].

Past Easter frost, no fruit is lost.

Late Easter, long cold spring.

AT ST GEORGE THE MEADOW TURNS TO HAY

One of several sayings relating to St George's Day, 23 April, which celebrates the patron saint of England. By this time of year grass, clover and other meadow plants are surging in growth, and within weeks will be ready to harvest as hay.

The identity of St George is something of a mystery. He was possibly an officer of high rank in the Roman army who was martyred in Palestine early in the fourth century. Certainly he never confronted or killed a dragon and equally certainly he was invoked as an aid to victory by crusaders in the 12th century.

The legend of St George and the dragon – and his association with agriculture and the fertility of the fields – could be a survival of the myth of the Egyptian god Horus, or that of the Greek hero Perseus. As Viscountess Wolseley writes in *The Countryman's Log-Book* of 1921: '. . . the dragon, named typhoon, denoted the desert or winter period of darkness. This dragon was slain by the Sun-god Horus . . . He became the god of the Egyptians, and his festival coincided, curiously enough, with our St. George's Day, for it was held on April 23. Then again, we get a somewhat similar myth in that of the Greek Perseus, who slew the dragon, or, in other words, winter.' It is said that 'There is no spring without George.'

> *Dragons have an ancient association with water. In medieval times river floods, prevalent in spring, were sometimes known as 'dragons' and those who were able to abate them were, like St George, heralded as dragonslayers.*

Who shears his sheep before St Servatius' Day loves more his wool than his sheep

That is, before 13 May. The logic behind the saying is that there is often a cold snap at about this time of year, so it is better for both farmer and sheep to wait until June before shearing.

For sheep grazing in upland areas it may be wise to wait even until July to complete shearing. Edward Topsell, the curate and author in 1607 of *The Historie of Foure-footed Beastes*, writing at a time when the wool trade was the backbone of the English economy, extolled the merits of home-reared sheep: 'The common time whereat we sheare sheep,' he says, 'is in June, and lambes in July; the quantitie of wool upon our sheep is more than any other countrey of the world, for even the least among us, such as are in hard grounds as in Norfolke, the upper most part of Kent, Hertford-shier, and other places have better and weightier fleeces then the greatest in other nations.'

St Servatius, a fourth-century bishop of Tongeren in Belgium, is one of the so-called Ice Saints, whose feast days fell during 11–14 May, traditionally (under the Julian calendar) a spell of cold weather. In Brittany, until the end of the 19th century, a battle was fought on St Servatius Day between teams from the provinces of Vannes and Cornouaille. The winners, it was believed, would be assured a good harvest. After the ritual was stopped, its cessation was widely blamed for a series of bad years.

ICE SAINTS

Apart from Servatius, the other Ice Saints are:

St Mamertus (11 May), a fifth-century archbishop of Vienne in France, was the founder of Rogation Days, celebrated before Ascension Day, to help prevent further calamities to his community.

St Pancras (12 May), the patron saint of children, was martyred in Rome in AD 304 at the age of 14. Relics of the saint are believed to have been sent from Italy to Anglo-Saxon England, and St Augustine dedicated a church to him in Canterbury.

St Boniface (14 May) was an Anglo-Saxon Benedictine monk, baptised as Winfrid at Crediton in Devon, who spent most of his adult life in Germany, becoming archbishop of Mainz before being martyred in AD 754.

ON ST BARNABAS, PUT A SCYTHE TO THE GRASS

That is, on 11 June, which should be the height of the haymaking season or 'haysel'. Hay is still an important crop, but not as vital as in the days when it was crucial for feeding the horses on which so many people depended for labour and transport.

Whatever the weather, it is likely that by early June the first crop of hay will be ready for cutting. Before the advent of mechanical mowing, this was a hard task. The grass was cut with long-handled scythes, then left in the fields to dry since, if stacked 'green', it risked getting so hot that it would spontaneously combust. During drying it needed to be turned by hand every couple of days. Finally it was raked into piles or 'cocks', loaded on to carts and made into haystacks. Unlike the harvest, labourers were rarely paid extra for working during the haysel.

The scythe is a tool that was certainly used by the Romans; it developed from the short-handled sickle, which has a smaller, much more curved blade. Using a scythe to mow hay is an art that demands both practice and a steady rhythm, so that the grass is cut in a series of narrow strips. While the scythe is in use it needs constant re-sharpening with a whetstone. In the Basque country, scything competitions are still held, speed being of the essence.

It is said to be unlucky to meet a load of hay on the road, but Sir Charles Igglesden, in *Those Superstitions* of 1932, offers an antidote: '– if you turn when it has passed and spit at it all will be well'

St Barnabas, believed to have been martyred in his native Cyprus in AD 61, is credited with introducing the convert St Paul to the Apostles.

Gather herbs on the eve of St John

St John's Eve, 23 June, is a day for gathering plants to protect against witches' evil powers. Both the eve and the saint's day itself are prime dates for predicting the weather for the rest of the summer.

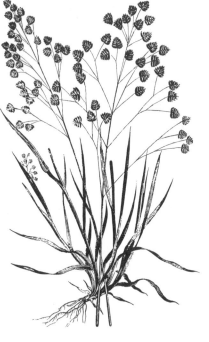

Although the summer solstice is on 21 June, Midsummer Day is traditionally identified with St John's Day, three days later. This is a time of year when crops and cattle need protection if they are to flourish, and to safeguard their future bonfires were at one time lit to banish evil spirits and bring clement weather.

Plants gathered on St John's Eve were credited with special powers, and foremost among the plants of the season was St John's wort (*Hypericum perforatum*), a yellow-flowered herb with a pungent smell; this scent is generated by oil glands in the leaves, whose red spots are taken to symbolize the spilled blood of the saint. When the plant was thrown on a fire the oil scented the smoke, through which people would jump for added protection.

At this season other protective herbs such as yarrow, mugwort and chamomile, and grasses such as quaking grass, were cut and hung up in the home and the cowshed. As far as the weather was

> *The pessimist's view of the British summer: 'Before St John's Day we pray for rain; after that we get it anyhow.'*

concerned, among the most powerful were mugwort, which protected against both witches and thunder, and elder, which, if allowed to get into the hands of a witch, would be used to stir the water in lakes and rivers to produce storms.

According to Thomas Tusser's *Five Hundred Points of Good Husbandry*, St John's Day was one on which it paid to be active on the land (brakes are ferns or bracken):

> *At Midsummer, downe with the brambles and brakes*
> *   and after, abrode with thy forks and thy rakes:*
> *Set mowers a mowing, where meadow is growne,*
> *   the longer now standing the worse to be mowne.*

THE SAINT AND THE WEATHER

Farmers and gardeners, in particular, would take note of the weather on and around St John's Day, because:

Before St John's Day no early crops are worth praising.

If Midsummer Day be never so little rainy, the hazel and walnut will be scarce; corn smitten in many places; but apples, pears and plums will not be hurt.

Never rued the man who laid in his fuel before St John.

Rain on St John's Day, and we may expect a wet harvest.

St Swithin's Day if ye do rain, for forty days it will remain

Relating to the weather on 15 July, this old saying continues: 'St Swithin's Day if ye be fair, for forty days 'twill rain no more.' In northern Europe it contains an element of the truth, as by mid-July the jet stream is likely to be set in position until late August.

The English poet and dramatist John Gay, writing in the 18th century, expressed the rule even more evocatively:

> *Now if on Swithin's feast the welkin lours*
> *And every penthouse streams with hasty showers,*
> *Twice twenty days shall clouds their fleeces drain*
> *And wash the pavement with incessant rain.*

There are plenty of exceptions however, not least 15 July 1976, when there was a violent thunderstorm overnight, and the most rain recorded on that date – more than 25mm (1in) – for half a century. Then, for the next 40 days apart from two, there was no rain in England at all, leading to the hottest summer and worst drought in living memory.

St Swithin, Bishop of Winchester from 852 to 862, may be associated with rain as a result of his deathbed request that he be buried not inside the cathedral, but outside in a simple tomb, 'where the sweet rain of heaven may fall upon my grave'. In 971, however, his mortal remains were moved to a shrine within the cathedral.

St Swithin's Day is customarily associated with the health of the apple crop, and rain on that day is said to be 'christening the apples'. It is also regarded as a turning point in the ripening of the crop, for 'Until St Swithin be past the apples be not fit to taste.'

> In Germany there is a similar day of prediction, 27 June, known as *Siebenschläfertag* (Seven Sleepers Day). Whatever the weather on that day, it will remain for the next seven weeks.

OFFER THE FIRST FRUITS ON LAMMAS DAY

That is on 1 August, the beginning of the harvest season, when a ritual loaf was made from the first cutting of the new corn. Before fields were enclosed by landowners, this was also a day on which animals were put out to graze on the hay meadows.

Lammas gets its name from the old English word *hláfmaesse*, literally 'loaf-mass'. From Anglo-Saxon times it was customary to bless a loaf made from new corn at the church and use it for a Eucharist service. On or before this day tenant farmers were also obliged to present a sheaf of freshly harvested wheat to their landlords. In Richmond, Yorkshire, it is still customary for the farmer who is the first to bring Lammas wheat to the mayor (as clerk of the market) to be given a bottle of wine.

In pre-Christian times, Lammas was a pagan holiday known as the 'Gule' of August, which may derive from *Gŵyl Awst*, the Welsh name for the date, meaning 'feast of August'. Lammas is also a cross-quarter day, falling as it does midway between a solstice and an equinox, and as such it was singled out as a holiday. In Scotland Lammas is one of the regular quarter days when, by tradition, servants were hired and rent and rates fell due.

It was once thought that burning ferns (probably bracken) at the beginning of August would have a deleterious effect on the weather. Writing to the High Sheriff of Staffordshire on 1 August 1636 concerning a forthcoming visit by King Charles I, the Earl of Pembroke ordered that no fern should be burnt at that time, 'that the country and himself may enjoy fair weather as long as he remain in these parts'.

Rain at Lammas time – but not thereafter – is welcomed by farmers hoping for a fruitful harvest. According to the old proverb,

> *A frosty winter and a dusty March, and a rain about April;*
> *And another about Lammas time, when the corn begins to fill;*
> *Is worth a plough of gold and all her pins theretill.*

At St Bartholomew There Comes Cold Dew

The signal of the beginning of autumn, and with it a change in the weather. St Bartholomew's Day, 24 August, was for centuries the occasion for a great fair in the City of London.

Around the end of August – once the 40 days after St Swithin are over – summer weather changes to that of early autumn, with cooler nights. When skies are clear at this time of year, heat escapes from the ground and water condenses as dew. But after a hot summer the weather can also break, bringing unaccustomed rain.

Beginning in 1133, an annual fair was held at Smithfield (the original site of St Bartholomew's Hospital) on 24 August. Commercially, it was important as the country's chief cloth sale – and representatives from the Merchant Taylor's guild would be present with their silver measures to test the lengths of cloth being sold – but it also featured sideshows, prize-fighters, wire-walkers, acrobats, puppets and wild animals. William Wordsworth visited it at the end of the 18th century, and described it as a 'Parliament of Monsters':

> If a stormy summer gives way to settled autumn weather, it is said that 'St Bartlemy's mantle wipes dry all the tears that St Swithin can cry'.

. . . Albinos, painted Indians, Dwarfs,
The Horse of knowledge, and the learned Pig,
The Stone-eater, the man that swallows fire,
Giants, Ventriloquists, the Invisible Girl . . .
All out-o'-the-way, far-fetched, perverted things,
All freaks of nature . . .

The fair was opened by the Lord Mayor of London, who would stop at Newgate to receive a cup of sack (fortified wine) from the prison governor. It became huge, sprawling across four parishes, and by the reign of Charles II had burgeoned into a two-week bonanza, but in 1691 it was cut back to just four days. In 1753, following the change in the calendar, it was moved forward to 3 September, and it was finally abolished in 1855 by the city authorities, on the grounds that it encouraged debauchery and public disorder.

ON HOLY CROSS DAY,
VINEYARDS ARE GAY

That is on 14 September, also known as Holy Rood Day or Roodmas, when it is believed to be unlucky – or even disastrous – to gather nuts.

By mid-September the grapes in the vineyard are nearly ripe, and within a week or so will be ready for harvest. At this time of year viticulturists welcome every moment of sunshine; not only will sunshine improve the sugar content of the crop, but rain in September can spell disaster if it encourages the growth of mildew.

Holy Cross Day originated as a commemoration of the day in AD 335 when the basilica of the Emperor Constantine, built in Jerusalem on the site of the Holy Sepulchre, was dedicated. While the basilica was being constructed, the Empress Helena, Constantine's mother, on a pilgrimage to the city in 326, allegedly discovered a cross, believed to be the 'true cross' of the crucifixion.

According to *Poor Robin's Almanack* of 1693, gathering nuts (nutting) needed to be avoided on Holy Cross Day:

> *The Devil, as some People say,*
> *A Nutting goes on* Holy-Rood *day.*
> *Let Women, then, their Children keep*
> *At home that day; better asleep*
> *They were, or Cattle for to tend*
> *Than Nutting go, and meet the Fiend;*
> *But if they'll not be ruled by this,*
> *Blame me not if they do amiss.*

ON MICHAELMAS DAY THE DEVIL PUTS HIS FOOT ON BLACKBERRIES

Or is said to spit on them – or even worse. By Michaelmas, which falls on 29 September, blackberries will, indeed, be losing their flavour. On farms, Michaelmas was the season for renewals and changes of tenancy.

That the Devil mars blackberries in this season is a long-held belief, mentioned by D.H. Lawrence in his 1911 novel *The White Peacock*: 'The webs on brambles were white; the devil throws his net over the blackberries as soon as September's back is turned, they say . . .'. Diminishing sunshine means the fruit's flavour fades in late autumn, and early frosts will make them mushy and inedible.

Seeds discovered by archaeologists in the stomachs of Neolithic humans prove that Britons have been enjoying the juicy fruits of the blackberry (*Rubus fruticosus*) for more than 4,000 years. Known as 'lawyers' because their thorny, arching stems are difficult to escape from once they entrap you, brambles were once commonly planted around graves, for the practical reason of deterring grazing sheep but also to keep the dead in their place and the Devil out.

Hired workers, as well as tenant farmers, would anxiously await Michaelmas and payment for their hire. In the traditional ballad 'The Jolly Pinder of Wakefield', the pinder (a local official whose duty was to impound stray animals), agrees to join Robin Hood's band of outlaws, but not until he has been paid for the year:

At Michaelmas next my covenant comes out.
When every man gathers his fee,
Then I'll take my blade in my hand,
And plod to the greenwood with thee.

If Michaelmas once more was come and gone,
And my master had paid me my fee,
Then I would set as little by him
As my master doth by me.

On St Luke's Day the Oxen Have Leave to Play

In other words, to mate. The competitive behaviour of male oxen – and stags – around St Luke's Day, 18 October, explains the origin of the 'horn fair' held in East London on that date.

The mating of oxen in the autumn ensures that calves will be born when the weather is warm and food plentiful. Among wild oxen, the horned males rut, or fight, for the attentions of the most fecund females. The sexual connotations of horns were applied to human activities in the notion that husbands with unfaithful wives acquired the horns of a cuckold.

London's horn fair is thought to have originated after King John, hunting on Shooter's Hill, seduced the wife of a local miller and as recompense promised her husband all the land visible from the hilltop – from Charlton to Rotherhithe. The fair reached its heyday in the reign of Charles II, when thousands processed from Rotherhithe (starting at Cuckold's Point) through Greenwich, dressed as kings, queens and millers with horns on their heads. On reaching Charlton the parade would march three times around the church of St Luke. The fair was widely denounced for its debauchery, and banned in 1872.

> Fine weather at this time of year is dubbed 'St Luke's little summer'. St Jude is often substituted for St Luke in the epithet, but on St Jude's Day, 28 October, rain was at one time always predicted.

When a blackbird sings before Christmas she will cry before Candlemas

Meaning that the bird may be tempted by warm weather in late December to mate too soon and rue the consequences in the freezing conditions of January.

The blackbird, a favourite garden resident, builds its mud-lined nest of grass in bushes and hedges during the winter months. On winter nights it is the last bird to be heard at sunset as it raises its whistling, rather raucous voice before settling down to roost for the night. These calls are quite different from the liquid songs of the mating season, which are almost concerts by comparison.

For humans, unseasonably warm winter weather means that the bacteria and viruses that cause disease continue to multiply – often with fatal results. This is almost certainly the explanation of sayings relating such weather to a higher than average death rate.

Like the other annual festivals, Christmas has its share of weather lore. Even the day of the week on which it falls can be taken as a forecast of the following year's weather, for example:

> 'Four and twenty blackbirds baked in a pie' might well have once been Christmas fare, along with roast goose and plum puddings, and mince pies made with meat as well as dried fruit and spices.

If Christmas day on Thursday be,
A windy winter you shall see;
Windy weather in each week,
And hard tempests, strong and thick;
The summer shall be good and dry,
Corn and beasts shall multiply . . .

And farmers did not welcome a full moon around Christmas Day:

Light Christmas, light wheatsheaf;
Dark Christmas, heavy wheatsheaf.

MORE CHRISTMAS PREDICTIONS

Traditional forecasts for the farming year to come:

If the sun shines through the apple-tree on Christmas Day there will be an abundant crop the following year.

If at Christmas ice hangs on the willow, clover may be cut at Easter.

At Christmas meadows green, at Easter covered with frost.

So far as the sun shines on Christmas Day, so far will the snow blow in May.

Christmas wet, empty granary and barrel.

If it snows during Christmas night, the crops will do well.

INDEX